Inspired Giving

52 financial teachings to inspire your congregation to give

by Shannon Pawlak

ISBN: 978-0-9700513-6-3

Acknowledgements

I would like to thank my husband, Sammy for being my cheerleader. Thank you for always thinking my voice has more value than I ever place on it. You are my everything! To my daughters Hannah and Selah, you bring more joy to my life than I could ever express. Thank you for listening to wisdom and learning from it, you both are truly smarter than I am. To John and Terri McCullough, my parents, thank you for raising me to honor the Lord first in everything I do and always being in my corner. I am not perfect but I know in your eyes I am, and that means the world. To Sam and Pat Pawlak, thank you for being the best In-Law's anyone could ever have. I cherish our sweet relationship and thank you for trusting me with your son. You raised a keeper! Thank you to all the voices and mentors that have come along in my life to help make me the person I am today: Miriam Reynolds, Pastor Carl and Alice Stephens, Pastors Sam and Jeanne Mayo, Pastors Gary and Rose Brothers. And thank you to all my God's House Orlando family, past and present for letting me share with you all these years! Love to you all!

Foreward

So you've just opened this book, and you're probably hoping you'll find some key or technique you haven't thought of yet. Chances are, you're well aware of the financial challenges of ministry, but you have an earnest desire to focus on helping people become more like Christ, rather than worrying about fiscal matters. You don't need a gimmick or scheme to alleviate the practical stresses of leading a church.

Here's some great news: you're holding a tool, a simple and repeatable tool that can help you accomplish both, faithful discipleship and financial instruction. And the best part; I know it works because I've seen these principles work every Sunday since 2003, and I've personally witnessed hundreds of new believers begin to trust God and the leaders in the church with their finances.

Shannon's perspective on giving, and her sincere care for the members of the congregation is a rare gift to a pastor. And I should know, I'm her pastor.

I pray that as you read this book and apply this simple plan to your services, you will find the way to guide your church to Inspired Giving.

Sammy Pawlak
God's House Orlando
Lead Pastor

Introduction

This book is written for any church pastor or leader who wants to teach their people about biblical giving. Good spiritual leaders want to see lives transformed spiritually, emotionally, and financially. No doubt, you take your call seriously in these areas. Too many times in church, we are afraid to talk about giving or finances in general.

The majority of local pastors usually wait until finances are at a critical mass point to teach a series on how to give or tithe. Many times, that giving series may end with asking people for a commitment to give to a special cause, such as a building fund or debt reduction campaign. Because we don't talk about it very often, people may feel pressured to do better, which can leave them feeling guilty.

It can be hard to ask people to give, and intimidating to convey the actual needs of the church. Compound these problems with the blatant abuse that many have witnessed from some TV preachers, and you begin to understand people's irrational fear that "the church just wants your money."

Over the last several years I have developed a proven plan that can dispel these fears, genuinely and gently guide your congregation to manage their finances in a godly way, and produce authentic generosity from your people.

I call it **Inspired Giving**.

Before I get to it, allow me to give you some background on my story.

My husband Sammy and I were on staff at a large church in Rockford, Illinois many years ago. Sam and Jeanne Mayo were the Senior Pastors, and my husband and I were the worship leaders. I can't say enough of how much we love these champions for Christ. So much of what we learned about being faithful pastors we learned from them. They loved people like I had never seen, and Jeanne was a mentor to me in so many ways, especially as a woman in ministry. She is my hero. Pastor Sam wanted to win every single person in town to Jesus, even if he had to take them all out to lunch personally to do it.

During a particular time of plateau in the church's growth, Pastor Sam and Jeanne were trying to tweak the services. They felt like they were running out of time for everything in the service. Not to mention, the weekly offerings were reflecting the stalled momentum, and falling far short of the necessary operating budget.

They asked some of their youth leaders to take out a stopwatch, and time each aspect of the service, from the opening prayer, announcements, offering, worship, message, and the closing prayer.

What they found was that the majority of time was spent on announcements, while offering and worship got the least amount of time. Jeanne had an idea. She proposed instead of teaching a series and asking for a commitment from the members, we as a staff would spend five minutes each service teaching on giving. Not manipulative arm-twisting or pressure, but real testimonies and encouragement on financial faithfulness.

It was amazing to watch what transpired. It was even more amazing to hear all of the pastors on staff at that large church take turns talking about their own experiences with giving. I loved hearing each of their different perspectives on giving, and hearing of God's faithfulness. We began to notice a positive response from the congregation, as well.

In 2003, Sammy (not to be confused with Pastor Sam.) and I felt God's call to plant a church in South Orlando. It would be a unique work to reach people in the Entertainment Industry of Central Florida. I can tell you if you think that employees of the nation's largest theme parks are wealthy, you'd be very disappointed. We would build a church of largely unchurched, spiritually messy, seasonally employed workers in a humble-to-medium income bracket.

To add to the challenge we had very little help from anyone or any outside organization. We did it all on blood, sweat, tears, personal money, and a lot of prayer. As with any startup organization, funds were scarce. We sat down and discussed how we might get this fledgling dream of a church off the ground with just a handful of suspicious members who were new to the concept of church, much less "cheerful givers."

The answer that we came up with has worked ever since. Of course, it took me some time to fine-tune what I am currently doing to be effective. We decided, instead of never talking about money in church, and taking an apologetic offering, we would talk about it every week.

Yes, every week.

Every single week we take five minutes out of the service to talk about financial management right before we take the offering.

It was intimidating at first. I wasn't sure what to cover, and I thought I would run out of things to say. I am amazed!

Years later, I still haven't run out of ideas and scriptures to encourage people to give. I was also afraid of what people would think. When I looked at it honestly, I was doing people a disservice by not talking about it. Money is the one thing that people make decisions with and use every single day. And it's the one thing that churches seem most afraid to address.

Did you brush your teeth this morning? You spent money on the water, the toothbrush, and the toothpaste. Did you put on clothes? I hope so. You spent money on the clothes you bought. Did you drive to work? You spent money on a car, insurance, and gas.

Everything you use to go about your normal day has cost you money. Once I realized people make decisions every single day with their money, I knew I had to do a better job educating them on managing finances.

Jesus clearly taught "You can't serve God and money." (Matthew 6:24) We realized that money had the potential to become a slavemaster to people, and could seriously hinder their trust in God. This decision to speak on the subject so regularly was intentionally made to dismantle the idol of money in the lives of the people we served. If they could see money simply as a tool, a means of exchange, they would be free to serve Christ freely.

I'll share more of my story as we continue, but I want to cover three things in this book:

First, we will take a look at what I call **Metrics**. These are the hard statistics of giving across the nation, so you can determine where your church falls in comparison.

The second is **Motive**. I will write about why you want your people to give, and why God wants your people to give? They need to be the same. It can't just be about meeting budget. It has to be about your heart and a genuine love for God's people.

Thirdly, I will look at **Method**. This will include numerous examples of how to capture the attention of the congregation, how to concisely convey your message, and contextualize it for your church, followed by fifty-two giving outlines ready to use.

Chapter 1: "Metrics" Because Money Matters

Before you ever start talking about giving on a consistent basis you need a clear picture of the numbers or the money metrics for your church? You need to know who is giving, and who is not. Perhaps someone used to contribute regularly, and now they don't give? Who are the top givers? Who are my lowest givers? What is the national average? How does your church compare with the national averages? All of this is vital information to know how to approach your congregation and talk about giving.

In our denominational upbringing, my husband and I were taught some things regarding pastors and church finances that may have had some ethical value, but they were not based on scripture. Here are a couple of these misguided rules: 1) Pastors shouldn't be in charge of financial matters. 2) Pastors shouldn't know how much members give.

Regarding the first rule, pastors are the CEO (Chief Executive Officer) of the organization. Their names are on the federal, state, and local documentation, as well as those held at the church's financial institution.

As the responsible party for virtually every liability for the organization, a pastor, most certainly must be aware and be involved in the financial matters for the church. Can you think of another corporation in which the CEO has no dealings with the financial well-being of the organization?

The argument is that pastors are spiritual leaders, and should only be concerned with leading the congregation spiritually, but I can't think of a single time that God has led my husband and our church to a particular direction that didn't have at least some financial impact. This is true regarding discipleship, worship, ministry outreaches, decorating, expansion, printing, refreshments, even toilet paper for the bathrooms, and baby wipes for the nursery. All of these things were required for spiritual direction and had an impact on the general operating budget.

We have been blessed through thc years to have capable financial managers and directors who are extremely adept at good financial stewardship. We lean heavily on these individuals for their opinions, wisdom, and faithfulness. But we would never be so irresponsible as to ignore one of the most important aspects of our church.

It is extremely wise for the pastor to designate trustworthy people to collect, count, and deposit the regular offerings in order to avoid temptation and to stay above reproach in the eyes of the congregation.

We also require multiple, unrelated people to complete these tasks together to provide sufficient accountability to this sensitive area. Nonetheless, pastors need to be fully informed on financial matters, and the best way to direct money. Granted, seminaries don't often teach these subjects, and we had to learn corporate financial management through other sources. If you are responsible to lead the church and its members, you need to learn to be financially wise.

The second rule about pastors knowing what members give is not a scriptural one.

One of the Bible's best stories about giving is in the Gospel of Mark, chapter 12:41-43. It tells of a poor widow who gave her last half-penny (mite) in a donation at the Temple. Where others gave large amounts, Jesus said hers was the greatest, since she gave everything she had. This account would have been lost to history if Jesus and His disciples had not been watching the offering.

The Bible does warn in James 2:1-7 not to show special favor to rich people, and treat the poor with contempt. I hate to say this, but if pastors could fall to this temptation, so could offering counters, financial managers, and church bookkeepers.

We don't use the information on member giving in order to show favor or rebuke, based on what we observe. It merely helps us to consider the level of commitment to the vision of the church. It may surprise you to learn that many times the individuals who have historically been the most critical and divisive, or who left the church with a bad attitude were never giving faithfully to the church in the first place. You'll discover that those who give consistently, whether small or large amounts are truly with you and are happy with the direction of the church.

The scriptural mandate is to not give special favor to those who have the means to bless you financially. We have had big givers and small givers leave our church for one reason or another. Being wealthy doesn't inherently make someone controlling. People with control issues come in every tax bracket. Treat people kindly, compassionately, and spiritually, no matter where they are in their ability to trust God financially.

Understanding the Crucial Metrics

The first question to ask is: **What is your weekly average giving?**

According to Relevant Magazine, an average American church only has 10-25% of the congregation tithe, or dedicate 10% of their earnings. On average, 80% of Americans only give 2% of their income, while Christians only give 2.5% of their income per capita[1].

That is nowhere close to a 10% tithe, which has been a scriptural standard since Abraham. The national average of giving per person is around $25–$26 *per week*.

Here is how you calculate that number in your congregation. Take the yearly income of the church and divide it by your average attendance, including children. Now take that number and divide it by 52 to get your church's average of giving.

Here is an example. Say your church brings in offerings for the year that total $200,000 and you have around 150 people average every week. Divide $200,000 by 150, which equals $1,333 that each person would give for the year.

Now divide $1,333 by 52 weeks, which is $25. This is your weekly average giving per capita/person. So across the nation, most churches have a giving per capita of $25 per person per week.

Here is the equation in numerical form.

Total Offerings for Year ÷ Average Attendance ÷ 52 = Average Giving Per Capita

This is vital information for you to know. Maybe your church falls way below the national average, or maybe they fall above it and you need to commend your people for being such great givers. Either way, this will help you to know your

---

1 https://relevantmagazine.com/love-and-money/what-would-happen-if-church-tithed

congregation and help you watch for giving trends in the years to come.

Another question to ask is: **What percentage of your congregation tithes regularly?**

I want to point out what I mean by "tithe" and not just "give." This is an important distinction. Tithing is what Abraham did to bless the Lord (Genesis 14:20). Jacob tithed as a commitment to God (Genesis 28:22). And it is what God required under the Law of Moses (Leviticus 27:30-32).

We believe and teach that Jesus Christ has fulfilled the Law, and we are no longer living under a curse. Just as we learn to walk in obedience through faith, we use the tithe, not as a requirement of Mosaic Law, but as a guideline for financial stewardship. Furthermore, it helps a church accomplish its mission of making disciples, and provides support for the whole community of faith.

In the Old Testament and New Testament, the term for tithing was "First Fruits." It was a predefined portion, dedicated to God from the best part of a person's possessions, crops, livestock, and money.

Special Giving is wonderful. We encourage and practice special giving for projects, missions, natural disaster recovery, and so on. However, the goal is to teach everyone to faithfully give a predefined portion as their "first fruits" to God, in order to give the first and best part to God.

We generally keep track of givers in the following categories:

$20,000+
$10,000 – $20,000
$8,000 – $10,000
$6,000 – $8,000
$3,000 – $6,000
$1,500 – $3,000

$1,500 – $0

Collecting this information will help you know who is actually giving a predefined tithe, who is giving above their 10%, and how many people are giving less than that.

Based on national income averages, and the affluence of your church's neighborhood, these are not too difficult to figure out. Givers who contribute less than $2,500-3,000 per year are either not giving at a tithe level, or are living in poverty standards.

According to Share Faith Magazine, only around 25% of congregations actually give. Can you imagine what you could do if that number doubled in your church or even tripled? Many churchgoers believe they cannot afford to give at this level and are never encouraged to try. Or worse, they are badgered and criticized for not being faithful.

My goal is to educate people on God's Word about finances, and encourage them to take steps of faith, which will bring blessing into their own lives, and ultimately enable the church to do what it has been called to do.

The last question is: **Who has stopped giving?**

I have heard money experts say "People before Money." If you see people only for their money, it is self-serving and uncaring. However, if you ignore the state of their money, you can miss a crucial area of ministry in their lives. Let me be clear. We have trained our Financial Director to alert us if he ever encounters two things: someone stops giving, or someone gives an extraordinary gift.

First, has someone stopped giving? This is the number one way to know if something is going on in a person's life. They may have lost a job and didn't tell you. They might be going through a serious personal problem, and giving is the last thing on their mind. They might have lost the heart for your church.

We have found that when people stop giving, and they are not in financial distress, they are getting ready to leave the church. We have even found this to be true among our leaders.

Use this to your advantage. Shepherd your congregation through the difficulties that come with financial matters. Find out if they are in distress, if they've lost a job, or are facing a crisis. Go to that leader and find out why they have lost heart, why have they stopped giving? What is the real issue?

You may be able to re-energize that leader by recasting your vision, or possibly putting them in a different role. You may catch them just before serious burn-out. Money is always the first indicator that something is going on in a person's life. Pay attention!

Secondly, has someone given an extraordinary gift? This can be an indicator of a new step of faith in a person's walk. If someone visits your church and gives a large amount, this can be an unexpected blessing from God. Thank the visitor for being willing to sow into God's work. Giving requires trust and obedience, and it is no small matter when a visitor demonstrates both in your church.

Perhaps a regular attender gives a large amount; this is also something to pay attention to. We will always reach out and thank them. Let me remind you, this is not giving preference or showing special privilege to rich people, this is acknowledging someone's act of faith toward God. People need to be commended and affirmed when they have done something out of the ordinary. This lets them know that you noticed and are grateful.

The New Testament has several examples of extraordinary givers (Barnabas, Lydia, The Widow).

We are not prohibited from knowing these unique givers, just cautioned not to treat them differently with our ministry efforts.

Equipped with these three Metrics questions — 1) What is the church's giving per capita? 2) What percentage of my congregation tithes? 3) Who has decreased or stopped giving? — you will be able to better minister to the financial well-being of your congregation. Once you have answered these questions, it will give you something to track. Watch as you begin to talk about money in a healthy way in your church how these numbers will start to climb.

Let me share our statistics with you as an encouragement.

Remember, we are a church of working-class entertainers, and people in the hospitality industry: There are no "rich" people in the church.

- We have never received an extraordinary gift over $10,000.
- The average household income of our congregation is between $40,000-45,000.
- We now have 80% of our church giving on a regular basis.
- Our weekly average giving is $46. That's almost double the national average.
- Nationally, it takes 6 months to a year before new attenders begin giving, but in our church, that time is 6 weeks to 3 months.
- We have watched first-time givers become regular tithers, and we've seen members grow in their finances to become business owners.
- Several of our struggling performers have become successful agencies, and are now

employing other church members in their companies.

My husband has joked for years "We don't want rich people to come to our church. We want our church people to become rich." People who trust God are generous. The more you teach them to trust God, the more faithful they can become. The more faithful these givers grow, the more equipped your church will be to carry out its mission. After all, money matters.

Chapter 2: Motive

The next important thing to think about before you start teaching on giving is your **Motive**. Why do you want people to give? The obvious answer is so that the church can have finances to pay bills and do the work of the ministry. That's true, however, I would challenge you that it may not be the best answer.

I want people to give because it will make a difference in their lives because I genuinely care about them. People can tell when you have a selfish motive when it comes to their money, so you have to care more about them as a person than you do their money.

When I started talking about giving every week in our church, I worried that people would think I was just out for their money. However, I was so convinced that if they gave, God would bless them. I truly believe in blessing that follows giving, I just had to convince them of that.

So I did something one Sunday that I have repeated now for many years. It was scary to say at first, and it seems counterintuitive to taking an offering, but I promise it's not. I frequently will say:

"I am talking about giving today, not because we need or want your money. God takes care of us and always meets our needs. I am asking you to give today so that God can bless YOU. If you are a first time giver, or brand new to this concept, I want to challenge you to give. If you don't trust us yet, you don't have to give here. You can give anywhere. A family in need, a charity you believe in, another church, I don't care. The only thing I care about is that you learn to give."

I was bold or crazy enough (or both) to take this risk. If I took away people's main excuse to giving ("The church only wants my money") over time they would learn they could truly trust us and be more inclined to give. And that is exactly what has happened.

Christy was a young lady invited by a friend to our church. In a short time, she accepted Jesus, attended small group, and was baptized. She started to listen to me teach on giving every week. It wasn't long before she trusted us enough to want to give. The problem was that she was struggling financially. Her job didn't pay enough, and she had bills that were stacking up.

One night after our small group, she shared her need and asked us for financial advice. First, my husband and I gave her a small financial gift that would help her pay her most immediate bill. Then, we shared with her the principles that we have learned from Scripture and the way we trust God with our finances.

We encouraged her to try something she'd never done before; to trust God by giving. Now, she didn't start by giving a full tithe right away. She started small. And of course, blessing started happening to her.

She got a raise at her job, so she gave a little more.

She then paid off some debt, and she gave a little more.

She then had money in her savings account, and she gave a little more.

It wasn't very long before she was giving a full tithe every month and became a huge believer in giving. In fact, Christy became the church's bookkeeper and financial administrator. Time and time again, she had a front-row seat for financial miracles in our church.

There were times when the budget was down, and extraordinary needs arose. God met every single need at just the right time. Christy has since moved away. She got married and had to move to another state. Christy still gives to our church.

Even with all the miles that separate us, she still gives. Why? Because she trusts God. Because she trusts us. She knows His heart, and she knows our heart. She knows that we care more about her than we do whether she gives or not.

I can also tell you about another couple I'll call D & K. This wonderful couple was with us for several years and filled many essential roles. They are mature Christians and amazing givers. They moved away as well for a job. But there have been several times over the years that they have sent us significant checks in the mail. They will sell some property, or come into a larger sum of money and send us the tithe.

I can also tell you about other couples and individuals who have moved away but still love to give to our church. Why? Again it's because of trust. Because we took the big risk to take away their excuse that all we wanted was their money. We earned their trust, and when you earn someone's trust you earn their heart. We've never asked former church members to give. In fact, we encourage people to find a local church to support and serve. The fact that many have continued to give after leaving attests to the condition of their heart, and the relationship they feel with us as pastors.

When you talk about giving, *your* heart has to be in the right place so you can help them get *their* hearts in the right place. The main thing that I am teaching over and over again is giving is about our heart, it's not really about money. Why do you think God asks us to give? I think it's because he knew it would be a challenging area for us to be obedient.

We all know that the Bible says "The love of money is the root of all evil." It's not money that is evil, it's the love of it. There is no better way to help your people keep their hearts in the right place than to talk about why God wants them to give.

People are okay with volunteering, helping out a friend, even giving to a charity at Christmas time, but the minute you talk about tithing they tend to get defensive. Luke 12:34 says "For where your treasure is, there your heart will be also." We have to teach people how to give their heart to God when it comes to their money. We also have to believe and trust that God will do what He said He would do. He will bless them if they give.

My husband and I were privileged to serve as music directors for Mikel French Ministries for a few years before planting our church. As we were preparing for our new calling, Mikel challenged us with a series of pointed, rhetorical questions. He asked:

> "Do you believe God has called you to serve the people who will attend your church?"
>
> "Do you believe that God will provide for the ministry to which you are called?"
>
> "Do you believe that God blesses His people when they give to His work?"
>
> "Do you believe His people will be blessed when they give to your work?"

Honestly, it was easy to say yes to the first three questions. But the last one made us stop and seriously consider the truthful answer. He continued:

"Unless you believe that God will bless others for giving to your calling, you should not ask for money. You will be asking from an insincere motive. Or worse, you will be stopping the flow of blessing that God has for them because you don't believe your calling is worth their faithful investment."

These words were heavy, and they took some time to sink in. We had to examine our motives for our mission, our conviction for God's call on our lives, and our commitment to the people we felt led to serve. I found that I could not ask people to give their money if I was not convinced that they would be blessed for giving. I could not ask people to support our ministry unless I firmly believed that I was obeying Jesus.

This is why motive is so important. If you are looking for a quick fix to get your church budget back on track or hoping you'll find a tool to make your members give more, you'll be disappointed with the results. Don't miss this: asking believers to give is just as big an act of faith on your part as giving is an act of faith on their part.

Among the entertainment community we serve, there are several motivated people who get up very early every morning, drive to meet a personal trainer, and pay money to subject their bodies to hours of strenuous exercise. Many of them speak of working out even when wanting to throw up.

I like my sleep too much for such foolishness. I also lack the motivation to whip my body into shape with this level of discipline. But consider this, these athletes desire a change in their bodies, improvement in their strength, and increase in their stamina and health. They have allowed an expert with the right knowledge to make them do things they wouldn't normally do for themselves, in order to achieve the desired results.

When you lead people spiritually, they are looking to you to help them achieve spiritual results they cannot reach on their own. It is your responsibility as a leader to lead them to what will produce the greatest benefit in their spiritual lives. Learning to trust God with finances is an essential area of growth for every follower of Jesus Christ.

Every teaching that I do is always centered around how this will make their life better. After a year or two of teaching on just giving or tithing, I realized that I had just scratched the surface of the subject of money, in general.

If you ask most people if they would donate to church if they had unlimited money, they would all say "Yes, of course." That leads me to believe if they are not giving, it's because they think they can't afford it. The best way for them to afford it is to become a great steward of what they have.

After I came to that realization I started teaching on everything related to their finances. Saving, investing, being debt-free, retirement, budgets, raises, inheritance, working hard, everything. Even our kids and teens learn about handling birthday money and allowances. I started to challenge them to get their finances in order.

If people feel they have enough money, they are much more likely to give. This opened up limitless topics and scriptures to encourage people on how to get their finances in order. God will bless them when they are in control of their money instead of their money being in control of them.

Here are some questions for you to answer as you begin to think about teaching on giving and finances:

- What are the preconceived ideas my congregation has about giving?
- How can I earn their trust?
- What is the biggest financial deterrent to people giving? (ie: low income, large debt, unemployment, etc.)

These will help you contextualize how to teach your people.

Chapter 3: Method

Now let's look at the nuts and bolts of how I teach on finances every week.

You may ask, "Why every week?" I think of it as a vaccination. Rather than waiting until you are sick, and then taking a huge round of antibiotics, and over-the-counter medicine to get better, you just get a small injection every week. Over time you stop getting sick.

I would rather talk about it all the time, and teach my people that giving is a positive experience rather than waiting once a year and running the risk of making people feel bad that they haven't given.

There are a few simple little rules that I follow. First, it has to be five minutes. From the introduction to when you say "Let's pray" should require no longer than five minutes. You don't want to overload people with information, so keep it simple.

In fact, most of the time I try to include the prayer in my five minutes. If you talk too long, you will lose their attention. Secondly, I follow an outline. This keeps me on task and makes sure that I don't go down any rabbit trails. Third, I always have *them* pray over their money. Not only am I teaching them how to give, but I am teaching them how to pray over their own money. I always use a three-point outline.

Title of message or Main Point

I. Attention Getter
II. Scripture
III. Application

The Title of Message or Main Point

I always try to base my teaching off a point from the pastor's sermon. I don't want to teach on having peace in your finances and being humble and gentle before the Lord, only to have the pastor preach about spiritual warfare.I make sure that what I'm saying goes along with the sermon.

I might not always do exactly the same point, but it will work with the sermon. Sometimes I even use the same scripture, or sometimes I borrow a main point or idea. I don't want people to hear two conflicting messages — I only want them to hear one message that day.

Point I

The first point is all about getting their attention. I strive to find a different way to do that each week. Let me give you an illustration:

If I'm going to talk about the power of the Holy Spirit at work in our finances, I might bring up a power drill. I would ask someone to volunteer to come and help me. I would have them use a screwdriver to put a screw into a piece of wood, then I would ask them to use the power drill to do the same thing. Then I would ask them which tool was easier to use? Of course, the power drill is easier. Using the screwdriver is doing it in our own strength, using the drill is like using the power of the Holy Spirit.

I will use almost anything to get their attention. Sometimes I start with having them finish a quote like, "A penny saved is a penny ________?". Or I might put up a photo of an object, or I will use an actual object. I will also have them call out answers to a question, or tell a story. There are endless ways to get their attention.

I have people ask me all the time, "How do you come up with all of that every week?" I admit I have an advantage. My father was a lifelong teacher. He taught high school physics for over 35 years. He had a knack for object lessons and little sayings that would stick in people's minds. He would create wacky contests and give away chocolate to kids who had the right answer. He would even dress up as a famous scientist, and talk in an accent all day.

I have friends from high school who still tell me that my dad was their favorite teacher and that he inspired them to go into science. I grew up watching him teach. He had this amazing way of taking something very complicated and making it simple. He would almost always have something in his hand to illustrate what he was talking about. He was, and still is, brilliant.

I am just emulating him when I teach, but I have to say, it works. Not everyone has an example to follow like I did, so I wrote this book for you to use and learn. Use what is in this book until you get the hang of doing it on your own and start coming up with your own illustrations.

Point II

The second point is where I introduce the scripture and relate it to the opening. I always include at least one scripture or bible story to tie everything together.

In most speeches or public addresses, orators will make multiple points in their discourse. But in my approach, I only want to make one, very clear, concise point, that my audience can understand, repeat, and put into action.

Occasionally, I might do a multi-week series on sowing and reaping, debt reduction and saving that stands apart from the pastor's message, but this is not the norm. We like for the congregation to have a clear theme in their minds when they leave the service.

Point III

The third point is where I tie it all together. The object lesson or attention-getter, the scripture with application, and end with a point of action for the conclusion. All of this drives one main point home. Then I end with a prayer.

We choose to take our offerings a little differently at our church. We don't pass the plate or have the giving kiosks outside of the sanctuary. We have everyone stand as an act of worship. I ask them to take their gift in their hand; check, cash, or their debit/credit card, etc.

I want them to have a point of contact for their prayer. I want giving to be very practical on every level.

If there are married couples, I ask them to hold hands with their spouse as we pray. I want them to be in agreement and actively praying together over their offering.

Then we pray.

I have a written, declarative prayer that everyone says out loud with me. This prayer is taken from several scripture references and combined from several sources available online. We have modified it to make it our own. We put the words on the screens so others can declare it in unity.

"I thank and praise You Lord for providing seed for me to sow. You declare that I am blessed. I am a cheerful and excited giver who sows into the Kingdom of God. The devil is rebuked for my sake, and blessings pursue and overtake me every day of my life. I have enough to live and enough to give, for my Father owns everything. All your promises are as good as done. By faith, I am expecting increase, abundance, promotion, elevation, and overflow. In Jesus' name, Amen."

Sometimes I will write a different prayer if there is a point I want to make, or I may pray my own prayer out loud and have the congregation repeat after me. After we pray, they will take their offering to the offering vessels (metal buckets), and the digital kiosks located at the rear of the sanctuary.

I teach them that this is part of the act of worship. When you willingly and joyfully "bring" your gift to the Lord, it is an *act* of worship. An act requires action, and walking to the offering vessels makes that happen.

Many churches are too large to have everyone move out of their seats and walk to the front or back of the church every week. But it could be powerful to have a special Sunday where everyone actually got out of their seats to bring their offering forward, even in a large setting.

There are a lot of ways to be creative in helping people connect their giving to an actual "act of worship."

Over time this process will become easier. It took me a few years to figure out how to capture everyone's attention and concisely drive a point home in under five minutes.

What a wonderful creative challenge to face each week. I actually get excited about it!

The lessons in the following pages of this book are already prepared for you. The 52 outlines that I have created over the years complete with an attention-getter, scripture, conclusion and themed outlines for special weeks of the year like Easter and Christmas as well.

Some of these are a series, and some of them are standalone teachings. It is my prayer that these outlines will inspire you to create your own.

Your church is unique and different from mine, and God wants to speak something specific to your congregation. I pray that this is the jumping-off point to inspire everyone to give.

52 Inspired Giving Outlines

I always start each new year with a three-part series called "Why Give?" Always, always, always go back to the basics. I used to think that people would be bored with hearing something so simple, especially if it's repeated yearly.

What I have learned is there is always someone new in your church who hasn't heard this yet, and the people who have heard it need to be reminded.

I may use different examples and stories to demonstrate a point from year to year, but I always use the same three main points on why we give.

I love to reiterate that giving is God's idea. So, right at the beginning of the year, when people are making changes and New Year's resolutions, I remind them that they give, not because this was the church's idea, but because the Lord talks about it in His Word.

Start the new year off right with an attitude of generosity and obedience.

Week 1: Tithing

Why Give? Part I

I. Attention Getter

"How many of you tip when you go to a restaurant? Raise your hands. How many of you tip more than 10%? Raise your hands. Now what is the easy way to calculate 10%? You move the decimal point one space to the left. 10% of 100 is 10. 10% of 50 is 5. It's easy. This is how you calculate a 10% tip, it's also how you calculate your 10% tithe.

II. Scripture

A "tithe" means a tenth. The first time the word is mentioned in the Bible is Genesis 14:20, when Abraham gave a tithe (or tenth) of his increase to Melchizedek, a priest and King. The Hebrews also called the tithe "the first fruits." It is the first and best portion of what you bring in. Each year, farmers brought the first tenth of their produce, and shepherds brought a tenth of their flocks as an offering to God.

The story of Cain and Abel is an example of how offerings, or "first fruits" were brought to honor God. The story in Genesis 4 shows us what kind of heart God is looking for. The Scripture says "Cain brought some of the fruit of his field, and Abel brought the best of his flock. Cain's offering to God was a begrudged tip. Abel gave a heart-felt offering which cost him something. God accepted Abel's offering but rejected Cain's.

It isn't about what he brought, it was about the attitude of his heart. God found Abel's offering pleasing. Cain was jealous of Abel and angry at God. Because of his anger, Cain killed his brother in a field. The first murder in the history of mankind was over an offering. Cain's heart was obviously not in the right place.

III. Application

People of all sorts may like various things about coming to church. They may enjoy the music, the atmosphere, the teaching, and even the feeling of closeness to God's presence. But, the moment you ask them to give, many think "All the church wants is money." Many have walked out of church and never return.

By teaching on finances, we are not asking for your money. We want everyone here to know the blessing of giving to God. If you are new at giving, find a worthy charity and give to it, or help a person in need, but start to give as unto God.

Don't just give God a tip, consider the motive of your heart. Next week, I want to show you what happens on God's end of the giving deal.

Week 2: Sowing and Reaping

Why Give? Part II

I. Attention Getter

(Put up a photo of zucchini, or better yet, bring in a package of zucchini seeds, or a plant.) Raise your hand if you have ever grown anything in a garden. One of the easiest things in the world to grow is zucchini. If you have ever planted zucchini then you know how easy it is, and what a large crop you get from it. One zucchini plant can produce six to ten pounds in one season.

II. Scripture

II Corinthians 9:6-10 says, "Remember this—a farmer who plants only a few seeds will get a small crop. But the one who plants generously will get a generous crop. You must each decide in your heart how much to give. And don't give reluctantly or in response to pressure. For God loves a person who gives cheerfully. And God will generously provide all you need. Then you will always have everything you need and plenty left over to share with others. As the Scriptures say, 'They share freely and give generously to the poor. Their good deeds will be remembered forever.' For God is the one who provides seed for the farmer and then bread to eat. In the same way, he will provide and increase your resources and then produce a great harvest of generosity in you."

This scripture is all about sowing and reaping, or planting and harvesting. If you give, God will increase your storehouse. The Apostle Paul wrote these words to the church in Corinth, Greece. He was speaking in terms that they would understand. They had to grow their own food. They understood the concept of sowing and reaping better than we do today.

God wants to bless you, pour back into you. He wants you to plant seed so that it can grow become a harvest. There are lots of scriptures on blessing and giving, I challenge you to look some of them up on your own.

III. Application

As you give your offering to the Lord today, you are planting seed. That seed is going to grow into a harvest of blessing. It is God who provides the growth. This scripture tells us to plant a generous crop and to do it cheerfully.

If God could make a zucchini so fruitful, imagine what He can do with your seed. God is going to provide all you need and increase your storehouse. The storehouse is blessing.

Let's pray for our gifts to grow as we give today.

Week 3: Obedience in Giving

Why Give? Part III

I. Attention Getter

(Tell a story of being obedient.) I tell the story of getting a speeding ticket and how I had to make up for what I had done. If I had just obeyed in the first place, I wouldn't have had to make up for the wrong I had committed. I knew what the law was. I was just having a good day and had forgotten to pay attention. The consequence was still the same. Doing something right from the beginning is easier than having to make up for it later.

II. Scripture

I Samuel 15:22 says, "What is more pleasing to the Lord: your burnt offerings and sacrifices or your obedience to his voice? Listen. Obedience is better than sacrifice, and submission is better than offering the fat of rams."

This verse is from the story of King Saul, the first king of Israel, and his disobedience to the Lord. God had given orders for Saul to destroy everything after a victory. Saul decided to save the best livestock, took spoils, and even made sacrifices in God's Name. God didn't want the sacrifices. He desired Saul's obedience more than anything else.

When a child disobeys their parent, a good parent teaches the child to make up for it. These are important lessons for kids. Return that broken toy or tell the truth, or say you're sorry. But a parent doesn't want to teach a child to make up for something. No, the parent wants the child to obey what they told them the first time.

III. Application

In handling your finances, you may make mistakes along the way, bad investments, overspending, going into too much debt, or refusing to learn generosity. All these bad decisions can be made up for. But it would be better to start off with the foundation that our Heavenly Father gives us. Obedience is better than sacrifice. Give today as a sign of your obedience, and blessing will follow.

Week 4: No Fear

I. Attention Getter

There is a lot of fear that people have about money. They fear not having enough to pay the bills, not having enough to buy a house, or not having enough to retire. Not being able to retire is actually one of my biggest fears about finances. This fear makes me overthink my future and causes me to miss my present moment. It can affect the way that I treat my spouse and my children because I'm allowing my daily decisions to be fear-driven. (Feel free to share your own story of fear concerning money.)

II. Scripture

I Timothy 1:7 says, "For God has not given us a spirit of fear, but power, love, and a sound mind." Raise your hand: how many of you have food and money for today? Tomorrow? Raise your hand. Next week? Raise your hand. Next month? Raise your hand.

How many of you are worried or afraid you won't have enough next month? Next year? Or for retirement? It is our natural tendency to worry and fret. We know we shouldn't worry, but we do. Let's look to The Lord's prayer that instructs us to ask only for our "daily bread." Say this with me: "Give us this day our DAILY bread." It doesn't tell us to ask for next week, next month or next year.

Matthew 6:31-34 says, "So don't worry about these things saying, 'What will we eat? What will we drink? What will we wear?' These things dominate the thoughts of unbelievers, but your Heavenly Father already knows all your needs. Seek the Kingdom of God above all else, and live righteously, and he will give you everything you need. So don't worry about tomorrow, for tomorrow will bring its own worries. Today's trouble is enough for today."

III. Application

These are the words of Jesus telling us not to worry about tomorrow, it has worries of its own. And the Lord's Prayer, as we call it, encourages us to ask the Heavenly Father to provide for our daily needs.

Are we to plan ahead? *Yes.* Are we to worry? *No.*

The truth is, I can't fully fund my retirement in a day. I make good daily decisions, which contribute toward my future. I won't let fear keep me from doing today what God has given me the opportunity to do. You can give to him today knowing that he will take care of your present and your future. Say "Yes" to wisdom, say "Yes" to generosity, and say "No" to fear about your finances.

Week 5: Worry

I. Attention Getter

Let me ask you all a question: "How do you know when your finances are in control of you, instead of you in control of your finances?" I am going to read my top 10 list of things we do when we are worried about money. If you do more than 5 of the things on this list, it is a good indication your money is in control, not you. Don't raise your hand if they apply, just see if these statements apply to you.

1. I avoid looking at the bank statement.
2. I don't open the bills when they come in.
3. I blame someone else when overspending occurs.
4. I panic when there is an emergency because I have no emergency fund.
5. I spend more to feel better when I'm upset.
6. I have no budget.
7. I have little to no retirement fund.
8. I consistently pay late fees.
9. I consistently spend into my next paycheck.
10. I worry about not having enough for the future.

"How many of you at some point in your life can identify with one or more of the 10 things I just listed? Raise your hand." Worry, fear, and lack are not from the Lord.

II. Scripture

Philippians 4:6-7 says, "Don't worry about anything; instead, pray about everything. Tell God what you need, and thank him for all he has done.

Then you will experience God's peace, which exceeds anything we can understand. His peace will guard your hearts and minds as you live in Christ Jesus."

III. Application

If the top 10 list is ruling your mind today, reflect on Philippians. Don't worry today, get into action today. Take control of your money. If you know you are making bad financial decisions then it is time to change that.

Step one begins with trusting the Lord with your finances and letting Him give you peace. Give as an act of obedience, and Ask God to be in charge of your finances. He doesn't want you to be worried. You can be thankful for what's He's going to do as you trust Him.

Week 6: Valentine's Day

I. Attention Getter

(I find and hold up a homemade Valentine from one of my kids, or make one for demonstration purposes.)

"Remember when you were a kid and you would make your mom, dad, or family member a special Valentine? Why did you do it? Why give them a special Valentine? Aren't the preprinted ones that you buy at the store good enough?

No. When you want to show someone that you love them, you go beyond what is easy, convenient, or expected. You stretch yourself and do something special for them. When we give, we are showing our love to God, and He wants us to give from our heart.

St. Valentine is not a biblical character. He is considered a saint because he performed secret marriage ceremonies at a time that marriage was outlawed by the emperor Claudius II of Rome in the Third Century, so he's considered a patron saint of love.

II. Scripture

Exodus 25:1 says, "The Lord said to Moses, 'Tell the people of Israel to bring me their sacred offerings. Accept the contributions from all whose hearts are moved to offer them.'"

III. Application

Today we have a chance to bring something special to the Lord. It's not always easy to give, nor is it always convenient. But love causes us to go beyond easy or convenient. Our devotion to God moves us to respond to Him. Our love for those in need moves us to donate to charity. Our love for God's people moves us to share what we have. Our love for the church and our fellowship moves us to support the ministries that are provided. Our hearts are moved to show Jesus how much we truly love him. Let's give to him from our heart today.

Week 7: Investing

I. Attention Getter

(I ask the congregation to finish this sentence.) "An ounce of prevention is worth a pound of… (cure)." (Sometimes I will give an example from my own life of something I wished I had just taken the preventative steps instead of waiting until something was broken to fix it.)

What does that mean? It means taking the small little steps in things today will prevent having to spend more money later in life fixing something that was preventable in the first place. This applies to things such as health, doctors and dentists, auto repairs, house upkeep, education, and retirement.

I want to take a moment to talk about one, seemingly-small, financial thing you can do today that will have a *huge* impact on your retirement future.

Let me share some quick numbers with you on investing. If at age 25 you invest $50 a month into an IRA with an 11% return until age 67 you will have $453,000. If you wait until age 45 to begin investing and you up that amount to $200 a month, at age 67 that number drops significantly to $163,000.

II. Scripture

Proverbs 21:20 says, "The wise store up choice food and olive oil, but fools gulp theirs down."

Being smart with your money and investing now is a God idea. Remember, during ancient times, grain, animals, valuables were used as a means of exchange. Today, we use money, coins, gold, silver as currency. There was a very real risk of someone eating their grain, instead of trading it. You probably don't eat your money, but we may waste our money on things we want right now, instead of using it to secure our future. This verse in Proverbs tells us the wise people save what they have for the future, but the foolish spend and consume everything that they have now.

III. Application

Today, spend some time to consider your financial picture. Are you investing in your future, or are you consuming it all? It's the small preventative steps that you take today that will safeguard your tomorrow. Let's ask God to open our eyes to see what we can change in our finances to safeguard our future.

Week 8: Debt Free

I. Attention Getter

(Get 2 volunteers from the congregation. Ask one person to hold out their wrists. Have the other person tie a ribbon onto their wrists for each form of debt that you will read off, and keep hold of the other end each ribbon.)

1. Major credit cards.
2. Department store credit cards.
3. Car loans
4. Medical Bills
5. House Loan

(Then ask the person with the ribbons on their wrists) "Who is controlling you right now: You or the person on the other end of the ribbon? The person holding the end of the ribbon is in charge. This is what it visually looks like to be a captive to debt.

At this point in time, the average American owes around $8,000 in credit card debt per person. The average American has 3.5 credit cards in their name. As of December 2018, consumer debt topped $3.8 trillion. How many of you don't want to be a captive anymore?"

II. Scripture

Proverbs 22:7 says, "Just as the rich rule the poor, so the borrower is servant to the lender."

We are called to serve one another in love, but It is not the Lord's will that we be servants to debt or slaves to a lender. God wants you to be out of debt. Imagine what it would feel like if you had none of these ties holding you down. What could you do? What would be possible?

Do you know what someone who has no debt does? Anything he wants.

(This is where I cut the ribbons and have my volunteers take a seat.)

Here are a few small steps you can take to start getting out of debt:

1. If your credit card spending is out of control - cut them up.
2. List your cards in order from lowest balance to highest balance.
3. While paying the minimum payments on the rest, quickly pay off the lowest card.
4. Reapply the payment you were making on the lowest card to the next card.
5. Let this process "snowball" against your debt.

III. Application

Let's pray today that God will help those of us in debt make a change. We want to be servants of the Lord, but no longer servants of debt. Take a look at your finances and make some changes this week.

Week 9: Special Guest Offering

I. Attention Getter

Raise your hand if you have ever crashed at someone's house before? Now raise your hand if you have ever been a "guest" at someone's house before? Raise your hand if you know there is a difference between "crashing" and being a "guest?"

When you "crash" at someone's house it is usually impromptu. It doesn't require anything from the host. We don't expect the fancy towels or that breakfast will be provided, do we? We may not even expect to sleep in a bed. We might just "crash" on the couch.

However, if I am a guest I am treated differently. There will be a nice bed with clean fresh sheets and a place to put my things. I've even been a guest where my host put a basket in my room with some bottles of water, snacks, and candles.

II. Scripture

There is a beautiful picture of hospitality in Acts. Paul and Silas were in jail for preaching. God sent an earthquake to free them, and the jailer got saved. Let me read this scripture and watch what happens.

Acts 16: 31-34 tells us, "They replied, "Believe in the Lord Jesus and you will be saved, along with everyone in your household." And they shared the word of the Lord with him and with all who lived in his household. Even at that hour of the night, the jailer cared for them and washed their wounds. Then he and everyone in his household were immediately baptized. He brought them into his house and set a meal before them, and he and his entire household rejoiced because they all believed in God."

III. Application

Paul and Silas gave the jailer something of eternal value. They taught him how to be saved, how to know the Lord. Today, our guest is here to share with us. They are bringing the word of the Lord to us just as Paul and Silas did.

In turn we are going to give in our offering to be a blessing to them. We want to treat our speaker today as a guest. They haven't come to "crash" here today. They are bringing us a great gift and we want to bless them for it.

Week 10: Money is a Tool

I. Attention Getter

(I like to bring in a screwdriver and a knife of some sort. I hold up the screwdriver, and ask the congregation to finish my sentence.)

"We call this a screwdriver, and it is a _____. (Tool). (Then I hold up the knife.)

"We call this a knife, and it is a _____. (Weapon). The screwdriver is a tool and we use that to fix things. The knife is a weapon and it is meant for protection.

We can either use our money as a tool or a weapon. Have you ever had someone use money as a weapon again you? Don't answer this, but ask yourself, "Have you ever used money as a weapon against someone else?"

II. Scripture

Proverbs 21:5-6 says, "Good planning and hard work lead to prosperity, but hasty shortcuts lead to poverty. Wealth created by a lying tongue is a vanishing mist and a deadly trap."

Anytime we use money to manipulate people or punish people, we are using it as a weapon. Money was never meant to be used as a weapon. God never intended for us to use money to hold over someone or force them to do what we want. Let me ask you this, have you ever withheld money from God because you were angry at him?

Think about that for a second. Have you ever said, "Well I am not going to give this week because God didn't come through for me." Whenever we use money as a weapon, it is because it is driven by anger, fear, and control.

III. Application

God asks us to do the opposite with our money. It is not a weapon, but a tool. It is simply a means of exchange. When we let emotions of anger, bitterness, and lack get into our hearts, then money turns into a weapon. Don't let your money be a weapon of mass destruction in your own life today. Let your money be a tool that God uses to bring you and make you a blessing.

Week 11: Give to a Need

I. Attention Getter

(I ask the congregation this question seriously.)

"If you knew there was someone here today who is in real need, and you have $5 or $10 cash in your wallet, would you give it? If you do, get it out of your wallet and hold it up and wave it at me. Now turn to someone on your left and ask them if they have a job, raise your hand when you find someone who doesn't have a job."

Then ask that person to stand up where they are, they don't have to come forward. Ask them their name, what they used to do and how long they have been out of work. (Then ask everyone to take their $5 or $10 and give it to that person. Allow for the few moments that it might take.)

II. Scripture

Proverbs 19:17 tells us, "If you help the poor, you are lending to the Lord, and He will repay you." The Bible is full of examples of giving to others that are in need. This scripture says that when we take care of others, it is like lending to God and He will be the one to repay us.

I don't know about you, but if I am going to lend to anyone, I want it to be the best investment ever. The Lord is going to take care of you when you help others.

III. Application

Today, let's pray for the person here who we have given this blessing to. Let's all pray that they find the perfect job and that they will be blessed. As we are a blessing to others, God is going to bless us.

(We have done this several times in the past, and it always blesses the congregation to be an immediate answer to someone's need. First-time visitors are also impressed with a church that would respond to a need in such a manner. Try it.)

Week 12: Grace (Easter)

I. Attention Getter

(Have someone share a testimony, or tell a personal story of getting out of debt. Here is my personal story.)

"In the year 2000, we found ourselves in about $20,000 in debt. We took extreme measures to pay all of that off the old fashioned way. We didn't take out another loan, or borrow money, or empty our 401K. We worked really hard, moved in with family, cut our expenses, and paid it all off in a year and a half. We really felt God's help to meet this goal.

Then, in 2008 we were investing in the housing market when it crashed, and we found ourselves, yet again, with debt. This time it was $75K. The first time was from overspending, failing to budget, and some bad decisions. But this time, we were trying to do good things with our money and fell victim to a bad market. We were not sure how we would pay it off. We considered filing bankruptcy when God gave me a great job.

It took us about three or four years to pay it off by working really hard. Both times the amount seemed insurmountable. Through it all, we never failed to give God our tithe and keep the commitments of our faith.

How many of you have a debt that you owe of some kind? The institutions that we owe money to have something built into the payment plans called a "grace period". How many of you know what that is? Even though my bill is due on the 1st, they give me an extra 10 days to pay the bill without punishment.

II. Scripture

Ephesians 4:7 says, "But to each one of us grace has been given as Christ apportioned it."

We have all been forgiven of much by Christ. We have no spiritual debt today because of his grace. There is a grace period that extends to everyone to accept Jesus. You may be in need of grace in your finances. By putting God first in your money, He provides wisdom, age-old principles for success, and He helps do what you cannot do by yourself.

III. Application

Today I want you to invite God into your finances. If you have never given before, let him in. He will bring grace to your financial situation. He will help you get free from debt, and bring you into blessing. Let's call on His grace for our finances today.

Week 13: Provision

I. Attention Getter

I have a backpack here with items that represent what we need on the journey of life.

(Possibly have the audience call out items they would need on a camping trip. Take out, one by one, items that would represent shelter, food, clothing, protection/insurance.)

Going on a journey without the proper provisions is a dangerous prospect. I wouldn't go through life without some of these basic essentials for living. How many of you can raise your hand today and say that you have all of these items, these basic necessities that you need in life?

II. Scripture

Genesis 28:20-22 says, "Then Jacob made this vow: 'If God will indeed be with me and protect me on this journey, and if he will provide me with food and clothing, and if I return safely to my father's home, then the Lord will certainly be my God. And this memorial pillar I have set up will become a place for worshiping God, and I will present to God a tenth of everything he gives me.'"

Jacob had an encounter with God. He built an altar to the Lord and knew that God would watch over him the rest of his days. Out of his own heart, his own faith, he pledged to give God 10%. There was no commandment given, no church asking him to do so, no TV evangelists asking for donations, nor a parent forcing him to give. This came out of his own experience with God because his heart was turned to the Lord.

III. Application

We are all on a journey. Life is an exciting, and at times, risky adventure. God is protecting and providing for all of us. Today as you give, remember what God has done for you, what he *is* doing, and wait expectedly for what he *will* do in your life. As you have all the items already in your life that are represented here in this backpack, give God the one thing that you have to give, your heart.

Just like Jacob did, you can let today serve as a memorial of your promise to trust God all the days of your life.

Week 14: Missions

I. Attention Getter

(Hold up a passport.)

Raise your hand if you have a passport. Now, raise your hand if you have used it to travel outside of the US. How many of you have been on a missions trip? Jesus told his disciples in Acts 1:8 that they would receive power to be His witnesses and spread the Gospel around the world.

This is still our commission today as followers of Jesus Christ. However, not all of us can leave everything to become missionaries. Today, we have a chance to help sow into someone else who is helping spread the good news of Jesus to a place that you and I may never go. And we get to be a part of that mission.

II. Scripture

II Corinthians 8:16-19 tells us, "But thank God. He has given Titus the same enthusiasm for you that I have. Titus welcomed our request that he visit you again. In fact, he himself was very eager to go and see you. We are also sending another brother with Titus. All the churches praise him as a preacher of the Good News. He was appointed by the churches to accompany us as we take the offering to Jerusalem—a service that glorifies the Lord and shows our eagerness to help."

Titus, a fellow minister of the Apostle Paul is sent to the church in Corinth with an offering in hand and another person with him. Many of the churches in the known world at the time were contributing to help the believers in Jerusalem to be prepared through a crisis of famine.

III. Application

Since the earliest times of the Christian church, believers have contributed to send workers and the Word of God to far off places. Today we have an opportunity to support one another like the early church. This isn't about the church getting your money.

We know you are generous and you can't respond to a need if you don't know we have one. Let's all support this work around the world as they go to do what we can't. This way we will get to rejoice and be a part of what they are doing for the Kingdom of God.

Week 15: Tax Day

I. Attention Getter

"We are very close to tax day. Raise your hand if you think you will get a refund this year. Raise your hand if you think you will owe this year. Raise your hand if you have no idea. Now, raise your hand if you made more money this year than last year. Raise your hand if the job you work is an office job for a corporation. Raise your hand if you work in the hospitality/entertainment field. Raise your hand if you work for yourself or are self-employed.

All of these fields of work are completely different and require different skill sets. My skillset is completely different from your skillset. God has given each and every one of us something different that we are good at. These skills are used to feed our families, pay our bills, and more importantly serve God.

II. Scripture

Let's look at Matthew 25:14: [14] "Again, the Kingdom of Heaven can be illustrated by the story of a man going on a long trip. He called together his servants and entrusted his money to them while he was gone."

And Matthew 19-29: [19] "After a long time their master returned from his trip and called them to give an account of how they had used his money. [20] The servant to whom he had entrusted the five bags of silver came forward with five more and said, 'Master, you gave me five bags of silver to invest, and I have earned five more.'

[21] "The master was full of praise. 'Well done, my good and faithful servant. You have been faithful in

handling this small amount, so now I will give you
many more responsibilities. Let's celebrate together.'
22 "The servant who had received the two bags
of silver came forward and said, 'Master, you gave me
two bags of silver to invest, and I have earned two
more.'
23 "The master said, 'Well done, my good and
faithful servant. You have been faithful in handling
this small amount, so now I will give you many more
responsibilities. Let's celebrate together.'
24 "Then the servant with the one bag of silver
came and said, 'Master, I knew you were a harsh man,
harvesting crops you didn't plant and gathering crops
you didn't cultivate. 25 I was afraid I would lose your
money, so I hid it in the earth. Look, here is your
money back.'
26 "But the master replied, 'You wicked and lazy
servant. If you knew I harvested crops I didn't plant
and gathered crops I didn't cultivate, 27 why didn't you
deposit my money in the bank? At least I could have
gotten some interest on it.'
28 "Then he ordered, 'Take the money from this
servant, and give it to the one with the ten bags of
silver. 29 To those who use well what they are given,
even more will be given, and they will have an
abundance. But from those who do nothing, even
what little they have will be taken away. 30 Now throw
this useless servant into outer darkness, where there
will be weeping and gnashing of teeth.'"

This is the story of the parable of the talents. Three servants are each given a different sum of money according to their abilities. Two turn it into more and one servant hides it in the ground. The point of this parable is that they all had something in their hands. They had each been given a portion of the master's money, and the master expected them to use it to the best of their abilities, to produce a return on his investment.

III. Application

We live in a free country, but it's not free to live here. The government provides certain blessings, and for those blessings we pay taxes.

In a much bigger sense, we all have gifts and talents given to us by God. Whether you're a homemaker or work a high-level executive job, you have been entrusted to do well. All of the money you have earned, you earned using those gifts and talents. Therefore, it all belongs to the Lord.

Today, let's give back to him. He gave us the talent to earn money, and today we get to give some of it back to His work instead of to FICA. The biggest difference is that when you've paid your taxes, that's all you get until next year. When you give back to God, He returns it to you in multiple ways. It's a continual flow of blessing.

Week 16: Worship

I. Attention Getter

(I bring in a jewelry box or any small box. Then I have a volunteer come up and help me. I ask the congregation to think of one thing they possess that is worth money. Then ask them to call out what that is. Have your helper write those items down on a slip of paper and put place them in the box. Possible responses include jewelry, antiques, instruments, etc.)

II. Scripture

John 12:3-7 tells us, "Then Mary took a twelve-ounce jar of expensive perfume made from essence of nard, and she anointed Jesus' feet with it, wiping his feet with her hair. The house was filled with the fragrance. But Judas Iscariot, the disciple who would soon betray him, said, "That perfume was worth a year's wages. It should have been sold and the money given to the poor." Not that he cared for the poor—he was a thief, and since he was in charge of the disciples' money, he often stole some for himself. Jesus replied, "Leave her alone. She did this in preparation for my burial. You will always have the poor among you, but you will not always have me."

This story took place in the home of Lazarus, a short time after Jesus raised him from the dead. His sister Mary, overwhelmed with love and gratitude for the One who had changed her life and restored her brother to life, responded in this extraordinary way. She gave Jesus what is believed to be her wedding dowry, a life savings of expensive oil. She emptied it on the feet of her Savior.

Imagine that all those things we wrote on the slip of paper were actually in this box. If Jesus were here, would you be willing to pour it at his feet? I don't ask this to make you feel bad. I only ask this question to check the motive of your heart. We see the motive of Judas in this scripture. His heart was tied to the money. Mary's heart was tied to Jesus. Jesus meant more to her than the year's wages it took to buy the oil.

III. Application

To truly worship Him with our giving, He has to be more important in our hearts than what is in our hand or what is in your jewelry box. When He becomes more important, then it becomes easy to release what's in your hand. Today, give with the heart of a true worshipper like Mary. What you have in your hand today is less important than Jesus who is in your life. Today, as you give, tell Jesus that He is the most valuable treasure in your life.

Week 17: Law of Blessing

I. Attention Getter

(I bring my beach ball and toss it out to the congregation. I ask them to not let it drop to the floor. Then ask them to pass it back up front again. Ask them to answer this question,)

"What physical law is it that makes the ball always fall to the ground?" (Gravity.) I then ask, "Can you break the law of gravity?" (No, you can't break the law of gravity.)

"In this space and time, we are subject to this physical law. What is the only way you can keep the ball in the air?" (Keep hitting it upward.)

"Would you ever get tired of always hitting it and keeping it up in the air? Of course, you would. Gravity is a physical law that God put in place when He made the world. You can't break it. You can work against it, but ultimately it will win when you get tired of fighting it."

(If you don't want to use a beach ball you can hold up your car keys and show what happens when you let go of them. Gravity will always take over.)

II. Scripture

We read in II Corinthians 9:6-11, "Remember this—a farmer who plants only a few seeds will get a small crop. But the one who plants generously will get a generous crop. You must each decide in your heart how much to give. And don't give reluctantly or in response to pressure. 'For God loves a person who gives cheerfully.' And God will generously provide all you need. Then you will always have everything you need and plenty left over to share with others. As the Scriptures say, 'They share freely and give generously to the poor. Their good deeds will be remembered forever.' For God is the one who provides seed for the farmer and then bread to eat. In the same way, He will provide and increase your resources and then produce a great harvest of generosity in you. Yes, you will be enriched in every way so that you can always be generous. And when we take your gifts to those who need them, they will thank God."

This scripture tells about the spiritual law of "sowing and reaping." When you give or plant a seed in the ground, that gift is going to grow or that seed is going to grow. Much like the physical law of gravity, it is a law that God put in place. Just like planting a seed of corn in the ground, it has to grow. You can work against it. You can try to do it in your own strength. Ultimately, it is easier to just go along with the law that God created. Keep your feet planted on the ground and give.

III. Application

This is God's law, it's not the church's law. This is how God created our giving to be. If you give, it will return to you. Once you initiate this law in your own life, it can't be broken. So start giving. You want to get this law that can't be broken working in your life. Believe that in time, what you sow, you will also reap.

Week 18: Witness

I. Attention Getter

(I have everyone sing the song from Sunday school,) "This Little Light of Mine" and sing the verse that says "Hide it under a bushel, no.")

I want to encourage you today that your money and the blessings from God you receive are not just for your own care and enjoyment, they are meant to bless and care for others as well.

II. Scripture

Matthew 5:14-16 tells us, "You are the light of the world—like a city on a hilltop that cannot be hidden. No one lights a lamp and then puts it under a basket. Instead, a lamp is placed on a stand, where it gives light to everyone in the house. In the same way, let your good deeds shine out for all to see, so that everyone will praise your Heavenly Father."

Today, I want to talk about your money and letting it be a light to the world. What I love about the scripture I just read is verse 15. When you light a candle, it not only shines on you, it shines on all those around you. When I hold a candle in my hand, it not only shines on my hand, but it shines on the hands of others around me if I'm close enough to them.

III. Application

The finances that God has given you are not just for you, they are for others too. I always say that wealth for me is having enough to live and enough to give. To not share what you have with others in need would be like trying to hide that candle under a basket.

You can use your money to encourage people, bring them joy, give them hope, and show them Christ. The ministries of this church donate to feed the hungry, support missionaries, assist with disaster relief, plant churches, and so much more. Whether you give through our church or help a family in your neighborhood, when you give you are using your money to be a light that brings Glory to our Heavenly Father.

Week 19: Cheerful Giver (Mother's Day)

I. Attention Getter

(I will pick out the oldest or youngest mother in the room and give them a gourmet chocolate bar or something sweet. Or sometimes, I have all the mothers stand to be recognized and give them a small chocolate bar or something sweet.)

I'd like to take a moment and thank all the moms for all the 'sweet' things they do every day. Why do mothers do so many wonderful 'sweet' things? Because they love us. There is nothing quite like a mother's unconditional love that drives her to shower 'sweet' things onto her children.

Mothers have a generous and protective instinct that's built-in. Their bodies grow a life within, they sustain life after birth, and they spend the rest of their lives worried about keeping their child out of trouble.

II. Scripture

II Corinthians 9:7 tells us, "You must each decide in your heart how much to give. And don't give reluctantly or in response to pressure. For God loves a person who gives cheerfully."

When you give to the Lord, give with a cheerful heart. The Lord has done many 'sweet' things for us, just like our mothers. He brought us life, sustains our lives with His own love, and watches over us for the rest of our lives. He demonstrates His unconditional love every day.

The Lord asks that when we give back to him, we do it with a joyful heart, not under pressure. We want to give cheerfully.

III. Application

Today, as you celebrate Mother's Day and give back to your mom for all the 'sweet' things she has done for you, take the opportunity to do the same for the Lord. Think of all the ways He has shown His love. Let's celebrate Him today for all He has done for us and give cheerfully to show Him how much we love Him.

Week 20: Pentecost Sunday

I. Attention Getter

(I bring in my favorite snack food and bring in an unopened box. I use Cheez-Its. I open the box and hand out a few pieces to people.)

There is nothing like a freshly opened bag of Cheez-Its. They are still fine a few weeks later after they start to get stale, but nothing compares to the first handful right out of the freshly, unopened package.

How many of you have a favorite snack that is better the first day than after it has been opened a few days? I will admit to you that it is hard to let my kids be the first ones to open the box. I want to keep it all for myself.

If you are a parent, then you know there are very few things we ever get to have all to ourselves, and this is no exception. I am the one who worked hard for it, and I am the one who should be able to enjoy it *first.* And yet, the Lord asks us to give Him the first of our labor, or our first fruits.

II. Scripture

Each year, on the Jewish calendar, they would celebrate this special occasion called "Shavuot," or as it is translated, Pentecost. It commemorates when Moses gave the Law to the Israelites at Mt. Sinai, and it also marks the Spring Harvest. It comes 50 days after the Passover and a tradition called "First Fruits."

This was when the Jews were told to bring the "first" of their crops to the Lord. They were not to eat a loaf of bread, a cow, or anything unless they had given the "first" portion to the Lord.

Exodus 23:19 says, "As you harvest each of your crops, bring me a choice sample of the first day's harvest. It must be offered to the Lord your God."

This took a lot of faith on the part of the people because the crops weren't fully ready to be harvested when they gave the first fruits. They had to believe that what was left over would sustain them the rest of the year. And it did.

God asks us to give Him the first fruits before we have any ourselves. And it is much easier to give my kids a handful of Cheez-Its first than it is to give my money to the Lord. And yet that is exactly what He wants. He wants the really fresh, tasty, first-out-of-the-box, handful of yummy Cheez-Its.

That is why I pay my tithe first. Before we ever pay our bills, we give God His portion. Otherwise, all I am offering Him is the leftover pieces at the bottom of the Cheez-It box. We are to give Him our best, believing that what's left to us will always sustain us for everything else we need. And it does.

III. Application

This week, make sure that you are giving the Lord the best. Remember this is an act of worship. Look over your finances and make sure you are giving to the Lord first, and that you aren't just giving him the broken crumbs at the bottom of the box. Your electric company never promised to help you pay your other bills if you pay them first, but God promises to do just that if you give Him your First Fruits.

Week 21: Loving Your Enemies

I. Attention Getter

I want you to think of someone who might consider you an enemy. Is there someone who you know dislikes you? They might not have any reason to not like you, but you know they don't like you. Or is there someone that you don't like? Someone who you can't stand to be in the same room with? When you have a name of who that is, raise your hand. I have several people who I could name.

(Tell your own story of a bully/enemy or you can use mine.) I had someone growing up who didn't like me. His name is Teddy Zanner, and he was the neighborhood bully. He called me names and picked on my friends. He would try to hurt my friend, Billy Martin. I would defend my friend by taking swings at Teddy with my metal Charlie's Angels lunchbox. We have all been treated this way by someone, whether it was in our childhood or adulthood.

II. Scripture

We read in Luke 6:32-36, "If you love only those who love you, why should you get credit for that? Even sinners love those who love them. And if you do good only to those who do good to you, why should you get credit? Even sinners do that much. And if you lend money only to those who can repay you, why should you get credit? Even sinners will lend to other sinners for a full return. Love your enemies. Do good to them. Lend to them without expecting to be repaid. Then your reward from Heaven will be very great, and you will truly be acting as children of the Most High, for He is kind to those who are unthankful and wicked. You must be compassionate, just as your Father is compassionate."

When you read this scripture, I want you to put in the name of the person that you could consider an enemy. (Re-read the scripture and put your enemies name in it.) I don't know about you, but now this scripture takes on a whole new meaning for me.

You mean I have to give to Teddy Zanner? I have to lend to him and not expect anything in return? Don't you know what he did to me? The kind of love Jesus is talking about is not just love in words but in deeds.

As believers in Christ, there are people who will not like you, or what you stand for. Their beliefs, convictions, and behaviors may be contrary to ours. But if we see them in need, we are to show love, not just in words, but in deeds. Care for the poor, not just poor Christians. Feed the hungry, not just hungry Christians. This kind of love isn't easy, but it's what Jesus said represents the God we serve.

III. Application

Give to someone who doesn't like you. That's right, show kindness to someone who may consider you an enemy. Look and see if they have a need and fill it. This is how we show true love. This idea doesn't come from a church, it comes from the words of Jesus. What an amazing way to show God's love to someone. Find a way to bless an enemy this week and see what happens in that relationship. Watch God turn it around.

Week 22: Blessing

I. Attention Getter

(I bring in any box of food that has the following message written on it "This package is sold by weight, not by volume. Packed as full as practicable by modern automatic equipment, it contains full net weight indicated. If it does not appear full when opened, it is because contents have settled during shipping and handling." I usually use a Nilla wafers box. I will have someone from the audience come up and read that statement that is written on the food box.)

Have you ever opened a box of snacks or a bag of chips and felt like you got cheated in the packaging? Obviously, a lot of people have, otherwise they wouldn't have to print this disclaimer on the box. The value being measured in packaging may be different than the value I'm looking for when I open the snack box.

II. Scripture

Luke 6:37-38 tells us, "Do not judge others, and you will not be judged. Do not condemn others, or it will all come back against you. Forgive others, and you will be forgiven. Give, and you will receive. Your gift will return to you in full—pressed down, shaken together to make room for more, running over, and poured into your lap. The amount you give will determine the amount you get back."

This is how they did business in the marketplace. There was no sign on the Nilla wafers box back during ancient times. After you rode your donkey home, and the contents of your bushel had settled, your husband or master would be upset if you came home with a half-empty basket.

The remedy was to take friends with you to help you get what you paid for. You would pay for whatever you could carry. So you'd fill the basket, push it down to condense it, pile more on top, shake it to make the small grains sift down to the bottom, then with your arms full, your friends would pile more on top of the stack you were holding. That's what it means "Good measure, pressed down, shaken together, running over so that men will pour into your lap…"

When you sow into the Kingdom of God or give your offerings to His work, He gives back in full measure. No settling has occurred, it has been pressed and shaken and is running over. The measure in which you want to receive is the measure with which you give. If you only want a little blessing, then give a little. If you want a lot of blessing, then give more. It's not our idea, it came from Jesus.

III. Application

Consider your standard of measure today. I want to challenge you. If you have been giving the same amount for more than three years, it's time to change the standard of measure. Challenge yourself to give proportionately more and watch your blessing increase. Those who are already giving know that it really works. If you're just considering giving for the first time, start small to see that God will be faithful, then add faith to your generosity.

Week 23: God Keeps His Promises

I. Attention Getter

(I bring up a volunteer and hand them two bottles. One bottle is plastic and one bottle is glass. I ask them which bottle is easier to break? The answer is the glass bottle. Ask them to try to break the plastic bottle with only their hands. I then give just a few seconds and then stop them.)

"What is easier to break, this plastic bottle or a promise you have made? The promise is physically easier to break. Psalm 89:34 says, "I will not violate my covenant or alter what my lips have uttered." Our promises are easy to break like this glass bottle. Aren't you glad that God doesn't break His covenant or His promises to us? God's covenant is like the plastic bottle: we can't break it.

II. Scripture

2 Corinthians 9:10 says, "For God is the one who provides seed for the farmer and then bread to eat. In the same way, He will provide and increase your resources and then produce a great harvest of generosity in you."

There are two promises in this verse: Seed for sowing, and bread for food. That means God provides money for you to give, and He makes it come back for your provision. The one stipulation is that seed is provided for sowers.

Are you a sower? Are you committed to giving generously? The farmer is committed to planting seed, not just eating his seed. He sets aside enough seed to plant in the ground. Why? So that the harvest that comes up will provide even more seed and bread. The moment that the farmer stops planting, and decides to eat all the seed, the provision will come to an end. God's promise is to give the giver enough to give, and enough for your needs. Enough to live, and enough to give.

God will increase, bless, and enlarge your store of seed, that is money to us today. This is a spiritual law. It cannot be broken because God won't break His word. Once He has set things into motion, they will come to pass.

III. Application

Today, as you prepare to give, realize that the seed you have to sow was provided by the Lord, and He will also give you what you need for sustenance. By giving, we are showing our gratitude for what we have, and demonstrating our faith for what we need. What you sow, you will reap. It's God's promise, and He doesn't break His promises.

Week 24: Honor (Father's Day)

I. Attention Getter

It's Father's Day, and I always like to honor all the dads. What does it mean to honor? Merriam-Webster Dictionary's definition of the word honor is: "To regard or treat (someone) with admiration and respect; to regard or treat with honor."

For all you do to care for your families, your hard work, your wisdom, your perseverance, we want to honor you. (I have the fathers stand and I give them a present to honor them. Or you could have them stand and pray over them at the end.).

II. Scripture

Ephesians 6:1-3 says, "Children, obey your parents because you belong to the Lord, for this is the right thing to do. 'Honor your father and mother.' This is the first commandment with a promise: If you honor your father and mother, 'things will go well for you, and you will have a long life on the earth.'"

We are here to honor our earthly fathers today. I want you to pay special attention to what this scripture says happens when you honor your father and mother. It says that things will go well for you and you will have a long life on earth. There is a reward that comes in honoring your father.

That honor goes beyond saying nice things about your dad. It means showing respect, listen and follow their wise instruction. Obey the good things they ask you to do.

Our Heavenly Father cares for us, provides for us, gives us instruction that is good for us. What does He desire from us? Affirming, grateful words? Yes, we call that praise. Honor and adoration? Yes, we call that worship. Faithfulness with our finances? Yes, we call that stewardship.

We give in obedience to our Heavenly Father, and He rewards our obedience. We call that blessing.

III. Application

Today, we offer our thanks to God for the dads among us. We will honor our Heavenly Father with our praise, our worship, and our financial gifts. He's a good Father, and He loves to bless His children.

Week 25: Faithfully

I. Attention Getter

(I like to ask if anyone here knows what they would do if they won the lottery? I ask them to come up and share quickly what they would do with the money if they won the lottery. Then I ask if it would be easy to give to charity if they won a large sum of money? The answer is usually yes. Yes, of course, it would be easy. Then I ask "Is it easier to give when you only have a little money or more than enough money?" It is easier to give when you have more than enough. It is more challenging when you don't have enough.)

II. Scripture

Luke 16:10-12 says, "If you are faithful in little things, you will be faithful in large ones. But if you are dishonest in little things, you won't be honest with greater responsibilities. And if you are untrustworthy about worldly wealth, who will trust you with the true riches of Heaven? And if you are not faithful with other people's things, why should you be trusted with things of your own?"

I want to talk about being faithful in the small things. It would be easier to give when you have more than enough. To hit the lottery would make it easy to give. This scripture doesn't focus on the big things, it talks about the small. The Lord asks us to be faithful in the little things, and then He says we should be trustworthy with worldly wealth and with other people's things. Have you ever considered that God uses money as a test to see our motives and our faith?

I started tithing as a young person when I made very little money. Giving $5 or $10 didn't hurt at all.

But as my salary grew, and my income increased significantly, those tithe amounts got larger, and I found out why people who make more money don't automatically find it easy to begin giving.

You might think that winning the lottery would make it easier to start giving, but most likely you'd have a hard time parting with such a large amount. This is why Jesus is concerned with the small things. If you learn to be faithful with a little bit, you'll find it easier to be faithful with greater things. If you're not faithful as an employee of someone else's business, why would anyone be faithful when you're the owner? If you mishandle worldly resources, you won't value Heavenly ones.

III. Application

Today, we give to show the Lord that we are faithful with what He has given us. We give out of what we have to give. We are not expected to give from what we don't have. He will reward us with provision now and with the true riches of Heaven. That is a spiritual blessing. Be faithful with the small things now, and prove your readiness for greater blessings in the days to come.

Week 26: Independence Day

I. Attention Getter

I have everyone stand and say the Pledge of Allegiance. This week we all will celebrate the 4th of July, Independence Day. We pay homage and allegiance to our country.

The Dictionary defines allegiance as "Loyalty or commitment of a subordinate to a superior or of an individual to a group or cause."

We are committed to being good citizens of our great country, and we are loyal to America. What are some ways that we show our loyalty to our country?

(Answers may be: voting, serving in the military, taking interest in our community, praying for our leaders, taking advantage of our constitutional rights, paying taxes, obeying the law, and so on.)

II. Scripture

Hebrews 13:15–16 says, "Therefore, let us offer through Jesus a continual sacrifice of praise to God, proclaiming our allegiance to his name. And don't forget to do good and to share with those in need. These are the sacrifices that please God."

This scripture says that we offer the Lord a sacrifice of praise to show our allegiance to His name. A sacrifice is something that you give. It also says to share with those in need.

We've seen many people from other countries who have come to America to realize the dream of living freely. It's an emotional feeling to watch proud people who have overcome many hardships to become citizens. Many of our citizens who immigrate to America know more about, and value more highly, our freedoms than some of us who were born here.

Living here doesn't make you a good American, it is valuing the things we hold dear, "life, liberty, the pursuit of happiness."

Coming to church doesn't make you a good citizen of God's Kingdom. It's showing your allegiance, loyalty, and love for God's faithfulness. We give Him more than our words of allegiance, we give God our hearts, our devotion, our obedience, and our gratitude.

III. Application

Today as we show honor and allegiance to our country, let's also show honor and allegiance to God with our giving. We can give today as a sacrifice of praise, and give our hearts in allegiance to the Lord.

Week 27: Treasure = Heart

I. Attention Getter

Raise your hand if you would say yes to these questions:

1. Would you spend everything you had to take care of a loved one?
2. Would you give everything you if you could spare a loved from physical harm or sickness?
3. If you have children in your life, would you cash out or trade everything you had to secure the best future for them?

If you answered yes to these then your heart is with your family. They are your treasure, not money.

II. Scripture

Matthew 6:21 says, "For where your treasure is, there your heart will also be."

Jesus made it so clear for us to see what our hearts were committed to. He showed in this verse that your heart and your treasure are connected. If you treasure your family, you invest your resources into it. If you treasure your career, you put all of yourself, your time, and your commitment into it. The way we show God He is our treasure is to give.

When you love someone, you value what they love. God loves people. He loves revealing His Word to us. He loves for His followers to be in unity. If we truly love Him, we will treasure what He treasures.

We have to make the Lord more important than our money. When we give our money in offerings, tithes, missions, charities, we are investing in what He values, and we are investing in what He has in store for us. We do not give our money because a church, a pastor, or a TV evangelist said we should give. We give because He is where our heart is.

II Corinthians 9:7–8 says, "You must each decide in your heart how much to give. And don't give reluctantly, or in response to pressure. 'For God loves a person who gives cheerfully.' And God will generously provide all you need. Then you will always have everything you need, and plenty left over to share with others."

III. Application

Today let's put our hearts into our gifts. I would do anything for the One I love. Just as Christ is our treasure, we give knowing that He will provide all we need.

Week 28: Budget

I. Attention Getter

This is a famous quote by Margaret Thatcher. Read it with me (on the screen)

"Plan your work for today and every day, then work your plan."

This saying is especially true when it comes to your money. If you don't have a plan for where your money is to go, it will surely go and leave you. Our responsibility is to take care of what the Lord has given us, especially our money.

What do we call a plan that involves money? A budget. This word gets a bad rap. When I say "budget," most people have a negative reaction to the word. It might conjure up thoughts of what you are *not* allowed to spend on, or it might be a word that is used by bookkeepers when they deny a request. "It's not in the budget."

Try to reframe your thinking of this word. Think of the word as "plan" rather than "budget." A plan simply means I have a roadmap of a really cool place I want to get to with my money.

II. Scripture

Proverbs 21: 5 says, "Planning and hard work lead to prosperity, but short cuts lead to poverty."

Planning is a biblical idea; this is from the Lord. There are no short cuts when it comes to your money.

Psalm 20:4 says "May He grant your heart's desires and make all your plans succeed."

You need a plan if you want it to succeed, so the Lord can bless the desire of your heart. If you have never had a plan or budget before, here is a great place to start. Here is a percentage breakdown of where your money should be going.

This is just a suggested starting point. There are tools online that can help you with this. These percentages are per month and can be easily calculated if you list all your expenses per month.

- 35% Housing (Mortgage, rent, utilities, HOA, cable, wifi, etc.)
- 15% Transportation (Car, gas, repairs, tolls, etc.)
- 25% Other (food, entertainment, clothes, gifts, etc.)
- 5% Debt (credit cards, department stores, lines of credit
- 10% Savings (emergency fund, retirement, rainy day fund, etc.)
- 10% Tithe (Charitable giving)

III. Application

If you don't know your expense percentages, look at your bank statement and put each charge into one of these categories. See how yours compares. Talk to God and find out what is His plan for your money. Good money management doesn't just happen by accident. It is intentional. Make your plan and then ask God to bless your plan, and see what He does.

Week 29: Time, Talent, Treasure

I. Attention Getter

I want to tell you a story. This story is about a woman named Anjeze Bojaxhiu (Anyeza Boyaxhiu). She was born in Kosovo in 1910. She had devoted her life to the Lord. While on a training trip to Calcutta, India she saw the poorest of the poor. She was so moved with compassion for the people she saw that she had to help them. She had no wealth of her own, all she had was God's love and a calling to help.

She began missions work there in Calcutta in 1948. She received basic medical training and would beg for food and supplies as she had no income. A few years later she established the Missionaries of Charity.

In her words, they would care for "the hungry, the naked, the homeless, the cripples, the blind, the lepers, all those people who feel unwanted, unloved, uncared for throughout society, people that have become a burden to the society, and are shunned by everyone." (wikipedia.org).

If you haven't figured out who this is by now, she is better known as Mother Teresa. By the end of her life in 1997, the Missionaries of Charity had over 4,000 sisters (nuns) and 610 missions operating in 123 countries. These missions include hospices; caring for people with HIV/AIDS, leprosy and tuberculosis; running soup kitchens; and offering counseling programs for families, orphans, and schools. Mother Teresa didn't have money. She had no worldly wealth, she just gave what she had. What she had was time and talent.

There are three things God has given to *all* of us: time, talent, and treasure.

II. Scripture

Romans 12:6-8 says, "In his grace, God has given us different gifts for doing certain things well. So if God has given you the ability to prophesy, speak out with as much faith as God has given you. If your gift is serving others, serve them well. If you are a teacher, teach well. If your gift is to encourage others, be encouraging. If it is giving, give generously. If God has given you leadership ability, take the responsibility seriously. And if you have a gift for showing kindness to others, do it gladly."

I've heard that teenagers have time and energy, but no money. Working adults have money and energy, but no time. Retired adults have time and money, but no energy.

Whatever your station in life, we all have these three elements to contribute to God's Kingdom. All of these have great value and are necessary in every church. We've all given our time to gather in worship today. Many have come early and offered their talents to serve from the parking lot, the nursery, the worship team, to the cleaning crew. And we all have the opportunity to offer our financial gifts as a blessing to the church we love.

III. Application

Some of you might not have treasure to give today, and if that is the case, then you have time you could give or talent you can offer. Find something to give to the Lord today, and let it be a blessing to His Church.

Week 30: Testing God

I. Attention Getter

Raise your hand if you have ever had someone dare you to do something? I remember on the playground when kids would say, "I dare you. I double dare you. And then the worst dare of them all, like in *A Christmas Story,* "I triple-dog-dare you."

I don't know about you, but I would usually back down from the triple dog dare. The Bible says that we are not to put the Lord our God to the test or dare Him to do something. But, did you know there is one place in the Bible where God says "I dare you" and it has to do with your giving?

II. Scripture

Malachi 3:8-12 tells us, "But you ask, 'What do you mean? When did we ever cheat you?' "You have cheated me of the tithes and offerings due to me. You are under a curse, for your whole nation has been cheating me. Bring all the tithes into the storehouse so there will be enough food in my Temple. If you do," says the Lord of Heaven's Armies, "I will open the windows of Heaven for you. I will pour out a blessing so great you won't have enough room to take it in. Try it. Put me to the test. Your crops will be abundant, for I will guard them from insects and disease. Your grapes will not fall from the vine before they are ripe," says the Lord of Heaven's Armies. "Then all nations will call you blessed, for your land will be such a delight," says the Lord of Heaven's Armies."

The prophet Malachi delivered this strong prophecy to the people of Israel during a time when many of the principles in the Law were being neglected, and the leaders of the people were corruptly leading in hypocrisy. In this scripture God says, to "try me and put Me to the test." That is a dare from God. God is so committed to His own Word, and His promises that He dares us to give.

Wise investors do their homework to find out if a certain opportunity is worth the risk of investment. The better the guarantee of return, the better the investment. God promises in His Word that trusting Him with tithes and offerings, *will* — not may, not could, but *will* — "open the windows of Heaven" in the lives of those who give faithfully.

This principle is so powerful that unscrupulous people and some less-than-reputable ministers have used it to try and manipulate people for their own financial gain. But the fact remains that God promised, if you give, it will come back to you. If you give to God, He will provide what you need. When you are faithful, He is more faithful. And He is so serious about you making the investment of your heart to His purpose, that He gives a guarantee, and says "I dare you. Try me, and put me to the test."

III. Application

Maybe you're new to giving. Maybe you have never given before. Maybe you don't trust God with your money. This scripture reassures us that God will take care of us. When we give He says our "crops will be abundant." That means our jobs will pay off. "Your grapes will not fall from the vine before they are ripe." That means He will protect our income and we will have enough. I want to dare you to take the Lord up on His dare today. Give, and watch Him pour blessings into your life.

Week 31: Give Willingly

I. Attention Getter

(I choose a volunteer and ask them to role-play briefly with me. All they have to do is ask "Would you give me a dollar, please?" The first time they ask, I respond in the following manner: "Well… I guess… if you *really* need it. *Sigh* I was planning on giving this to the poor today, but… okay." (I will show myself really unwilling to give it to them.

(Then I will have them ask me a second time. This time I will say, "Absolutely. I would love to give this to you. Is there anything else you need?" I want to make the point that there is a difference in giving begrudgingly, and giving willingly.)

II. Scripture

I Chronicles 29: 6-9 reminds us "Then the family leaders, the leaders of the tribes of Israel, the generals and captains of the army, and the king's administrative officers all gave willingly. For the construction of the Temple of God, they gave about 188 tons of gold, 10,000 gold coins, 375 tons of silver, 675 tons of bronze, and 3,750 tons of iron. They also contributed numerous precious stones, which were deposited in the treasury of the house of the Lord under the care of Jehiel, a descendant of Gershon. The people rejoiced over the offerings, for they had given freely and wholeheartedly to the Lord, and King David was filled with joy."

When the Israelites were building the temple, they brought their offerings to be used, and they brought them willingly. They were so unified in their effort and so committed to their cause of building a sanctuary to worship God, they gave with generosity and joy. They also believed that God would bless their efforts, and reward their giving.

When we give our offerings together, we do it because we have a shared purpose to make a place where Christ is honored in our city, we are committed to being a blessing with our resources, and we believe that God blesses our efforts, and rewards our faithfulness. When you give for the right reason, you know the joy of giving. We give willingly, and we give with a cheerful heart.

III. Application

Let's bring our gifts willingly to the Lord today, and rejoice over them. As you pray over your offering today, check the motive of your heart. Make sure that you are not bringing your gift begrudgingly, but instead willingly to the Lord.

Week 32: How to Get a Reward from God

I. Attention Getter

Raise your hand if you like someone who is very accomplished, and name-drops, and brags about themselves constantly. Ok, raise your hand if you like someone who is humble about what they have accomplished?

No one really likes a boastful person, do they? What's worse is someone who does things only to look good to others. Humility is a much more attractive attribute in humans.

II. Scripture

Matthew 6:1-4 says, "Watch out. Don't do your good deeds publicly, to be admired by others, for you will lose the reward from your Father in Heaven. When you give to someone in need, don't do as the hypocrites do—blowing trumpets in the synagogues and streets to call attention to their acts of charity. I tell you the truth, they have received all the reward they will ever get. But when you give to someone in need, don't let your left hand know what your right hand is doing. Give your gifts in private, and your Father, who sees everything, will reward you."

There is something that happens when you give your gifts in secret. If you have given a personal gift to a person and they know about it, they will credit you with the gift. However, if they don't know it was you, the chances of them giving the credit to God are much higher. A gift is only a true gift if it has no ulterior motives. We don't give for the credit, or for someone to reciprocate. We give as an act of love and faith, humbly trusting God to provide enough to live, and enough to give.

Don't get me wrong, there's nothing wrong with letting someone know that you have given them a gift, but there is a mysterious joy and blessing when giving in secret.

III. Application

As a church, we guard the security and anonymity of our givers, and no one is given control of the ministries because of their generosity. We want every giver to know the joy of giving in secret and be blessed by the Father, who sees our gifts and our hearts. Know today that when we DO give in secret. Our Heavenly Father sees it and will reward us.

Week 33: Small Things

I. Attention Getter

What is smaller, a quiz or a test? What is smaller, a weekly assignment or a term paper? What is smaller, a test or a final exam? What is smaller, your daily grade or your final grade? What is smaller, a single class or an entire semester of classes? What is smaller a year of classes or a degree?

If you have ever been to college, most of the time when you take a class you can do all the homework, write the papers, do well on the quizzes, and bomb the exam and you will still get a great grade in the class. Small things seem insignificant until we add them all up into one large thing.

II. Scripture

Luke 16: 10-12 says, "If you are faithful in little things, you will be faithful in large ones. But if you are dishonest in little things, you won't be honest with greater responsibilities. And if you are untrustworthy about worldly wealth, who will trust you with the true riches of Heaven? And if you are not faithful with other people's things, why should you be trusted with things of your own?"

God is testing us in the small things to see if we will be responsible with larger things. God is asking us to pass the quiz, write the summary and show up for class. Then He will bring on the exam, and the degree but not until we have passed the test of giving.

Some people keep living the same existence, year after year, never seeing any progress. It's generally because we fail to pay attention to the important small things. One of the most effective things you can do with your finances is to make a budget or plan for your spending and saving.

It's a small thing, but it makes a huge impact on what you will have one day. Part of that simple plan includes giving to God. It's such a small amount in comparison to everything else we have, and yet it has such a huge impact on your overall financial happiness.

III. Application

Pass the test today. Be faithful with the small things. If you have never given before, start. If you don't give a full tithe or 10%, challenge yourself to give a little more than you have. If you tithe faithfully, look for more ways to be a blessing to others. Don't expect to pass the big exams, if you're not studying for the little quizzes. True riches of Heaven await you.

Week 34: Financial Advice/ Wisdom

I. Attention Getter

We have all heard bad financial advice through the years and good financial advice. Let's play a little game. I am going to read to you some financial advice and I want you to tell me whether it is good or bad advice. Would you listen to it or would you not listen to it? I will ask you after each one to raise your hand if you think it is good advice.

1. You should put away at least 15% of your income into a retirement fund?
2. You should have at least three months of income saved for emergencies?
3. When you don't have enough to pay your bills you should just stop paying on all of them and enjoy spending what you do have?
4. If you use a credit card, you should pay off the balance every month?
5. The first thing you should do when you are in financial trouble is cash in your 401K.

(Numbers 3 and 5 are bad financial advice.)

The questions above were pretty simple to answer. Why? These questions were easy for you to answer because you have probably heard good wisdom concerning financial management.

II. Scripture

Psalm 119:18 says, "Open my eyes to see the wonderful truths in your instructions."

According to Forbes Magazine, the Bible mentions money over 800 times. God's word has the best wisdom for your finances. The Book of Proverbs alone covers such financial topics as saving, borrowing, lending, debt, investment, and generosity. The Proverbs are full of instructions and wise sayings.

Not only is there a wealth of wisdom in the Bible about handling finances, it still stands the test of time. Modern currency, cultural changes, and new technology have not been able to nullify a single financial principle, even though they were written thousands of years ago. God wants you to be wise when it comes to your money. He is the best source to listen to for advice.

III. Application

Take some time this week to find out what God has to say about your money. What does the Bible say? Take some time to read through Proverbs and underline all the scriptures that talk about work, saving, loaning, borrowing, and inheritance. Be wise with your money by following the best advice ever.

Week 35: Contentment

I. Attention Getter

I want to read to you an excerpt from fortune.com. This article from 2015 was addressing how a great number of people who win the lottery usually go bankrupt.

"Indeed, the Certified Financial Planner Board of Standards says nearly a third of lottery winners declare bankruptcy—meaning they were worse off than before they became rich. Other studies show that lottery winners frequently become estranged from family and friends, and incur a greater incidence of depression, drug and alcohol abuse, divorce, and suicide than the average American. No wonder financial planners joke that if you have enemies, give 'em a lottery ticket."

Some other sites report that bankruptcy among lottery winners is as high as 80%. But isn't winning the lottery a good thing? It can be, let me read you a scripture.

II. Scripture

Proverbs 30:7-9: "O God, I beg two favors from you; let me have them before I die. First, help me never to tell a lie. Second, give me neither poverty nor riches. Give me just enough to satisfy my needs. For if I grow rich, I may deny you and say, 'Who is the Lord?' And if I am too poor, I may steal, and thus insult God's Holy Name."

I love this scripture, and we don't hear it talked about very often.

Remember, Proverbs is a book of wisdom from King Solomon, the wisest King in history. Multiple times Solomon advises against pursuing quick riches. We are not supposed to pray that we win the lottery and get rich quickly, we are encouraged to pray that the Lord will satisfy our needs.

I can even point to the Lords' prayer where Jesus tells us to pray "Give us this day our daily bread." That is a prayer asking for our needs to be met.

Now, is it wrong to be rich or to win the lottery? There are some that say that gambling in any form is a sin, but there is no explicit scripture against games of chance, including the lottery.

The prevailing wisdom is that throwing away money foolishly, and seeking excessive wealth are traps to be avoided by those who trust God's wisdom for their life's provision.

The point I am making is that most of us will never win the lottery, and there is no guarantee of winning anything by chance. But for those who are faithful with their finances, patiently working, saving, giving, these people will be blessed, and reap what they sow.

III. Application

Let us pray today that the Lord will meet our needs. Let's ask Him to help us be content with what we have. We don't want too little, and we don't want too much. I define the word abundance as having "enough to live, and enough to give." Let's pray for abundance and contentment today, and put the Lord at the center of our money.

Week 36: Kindness

I. Attention Getter

Have you ever heard of RAK? It stands for Random Acts of Kindness. How many of you can raise your hand and say you regularly practice this?

(Tell a personal story of doing your favorite Random Act of Kindness. "When I lived in Chicago as a young lady, back when you had to pay cash for tolls, there was no electronic device that automatically paid it for you. I liked to pay tolls for 5 to 10 people behind me. Tolls were maybe five cents or fifteen cents apiece. I would watch as I slowly drove away in my rearview mirror. I would watch someone hand money to the attendant, and then slowly bring their hand back in the car as their money was refused, and an explanation given. Then, I would see a gesture of thank you and watch them pull away.")

Your money is a tool to show kindness to others, and to God. Having a poverty mentality is when money is used only for your own survival. Money is a means of exchange, and a tool for your provision, and for blessing others. When you release it from your hand, it goes out to be a blessing, but in God's plan, it comes back around to bless you. Look for ways to bless others, even in small ways. The gift may be small, but the act may result in a big blessing to someone else.

II. Scripture

Galatians 6:7-10 says, "Don't be misled—you cannot mock the justice of God. You will always harvest what you plant. Those who live only to satisfy their own sinful nature will harvest decay and death from that sinful nature. But those who live to please the Spirit will harvest everlasting life from the Spirit. So let's not get tired of doing what is good. At just the right time we will reap a harvest of blessing if we don't give up. Therefore, whenever we have the opportunity, we should do good to everyone—especially to those in the family of faith."

III. Application

Don't get tired of giving. Don't get tired of doing good. This scripture says that we will harvest what we plant, so let's plant kindness.

This week, look for a way to do a Random Act of Kindness for someone. You could pay a water bill, pay for groceries, pay a toll, pay someone's dry cleaning, give a school teacher money for her classroom.

It doesn't have to be a huge financial investment, just a small act of kindness. Mow a neighbor's lawn, give some freshly baked cookies, or take some flowers to someone. Today, as you give, know that you are being obedient and kind to the Lord, and you will reap back what you give to Him and to those in the family of faith.

Week 37: Multiplication

I. Attention Getter

Today, I want to talk about God's calculator. I want to talk about the principle of multiplication. Answer this for me: If I start out with 2 sandwiches and those two sandwiches become 5,000, how many times is 2 multiplied to get to 5,000? (2,500.)

Okay, and if I have 5 loaves of bread and those become 5,000 loaves of bread. How many times are those 5 loaves of bread multiplied to become 5,000? (1,000.)

I am, of course referring to the story of Jesus multiplying fish and bread in Mark 6.

II. Scripture

Mark 6:41-44 says, "Jesus took the five loaves and two fish, looked up toward Heaven, and blessed them. Then, breaking the loaves into pieces, he kept giving the bread to the disciples so they could distribute it to the people. He also divided the fish for everyone to share. They all ate as much as they wanted, and afterward, the disciples picked up twelve baskets of leftover bread and fish. A total of 5,000 men and their families were fed."

We see in this story that Jesus took five loaves of bread and two fish, and fed 5,000 people with it. And afterward, there were an *additional* twelve baskets left over.

Investors research an opportunity, they look into the demand in the market, the cost of materials, the competition's share, then they do the numbers to see what their conservative potential for a return on their investment.

As givers, we also consider what we have, what we owe, what we can afford to give, and believe that we will be blessed for giving. But there's a big difference between a worldly investment and a spiritual seed. That difference is God's multiplication. He has the ability to take the little we give and make it become more to the hands that receive it, *and* more to the hands that gave it. All four of the Gospels tell the same story, but John reveals that the bread and fish came from a young boy.

Preachers have speculated that the twelve baskets left over were so each of the disciples could be abundantly blessed, but they didn't have the faith that Jesus could do it. It's my opinion that the little boy who sowed the seed reaped the harvest, and the twelve disciples had to carry a basket each back to his house, as proof of the power of faith in Jesus.

When your seed is in the hands of God there is no limit to what it can be multiplied to. Throw out your calculator, and don't try to figure it out. Only He can make that happen. When you give in faith, He multiplies it to more than you could figure.

III. Application

Someone there in the crowd had to let go of what they had in their hand and give it to the Master. The increase then not only benefited them but others. When you give today you let go of what you have in your hand today, and you put it in the Master's hand, He will use his calculator to multiply it back to you.

Week 38: Love of Money

I. Attention Getter

(I pick someone out of the congregation to help me. I hold up five $1 bills for a total of $5. Ask the volunteer a question.)

Which is harder, take this $5 and you have to give $3 to someone that you don't like, or not take the money at all? (Answers may vary, but most would say giving to someone they don't like is harder.)

For most people, giving a portion of it to someone we don't like is harder. The way we operate with money is based on our feelings. Your heart is connected to your finances. It is a heart issue. The money doesn't care if it goes to a mean person or a nice person. We are the ones that ascribe emotional value to our money.

It is scientifically proven that your mood affects your thoughts and decision-making process. It very hard to give money without assigning emotion to it. You can gauge this by considering how paying bills makes you feel. If you are paying off an instrument you've always wanted, or a ring you picked out for a special occasion, you might have less of a negative response the bill comes due. Why? Because you wanted that item and you're still committed to paying it off.

However, if you are facing a lot of credit card debt, or a second mortgage for something you don't have anymore, you'll have a negative reaction every month when you pay the bill.

II. Scripture

I Timothy 6:9-10 says, "But people who long to be rich fall into temptation, and are trapped by many foolish and harmful desires that plunge them into ruin and destruction. For the love of money is the root of all kinds of evil. And some people, craving money, have wandered from the true faith and pierced themselves with many sorrows."

This verse is often misquoted. Some will wrongfully say "Money is the root of all evil." Money in and of itself is not evil. It is the love of money that is a cause for caution.

We get into trouble when we give our money emotional power. How do you react when it's time to take an offering? Do you feel resentment? Has something happened in the past that makes you want to punish the church you attend by withholding your offering? Is giving money to God and His work, just another bill to resent?

Or have you experienced the blessing of faithful giving? Do you look forward to obeying God with your offerings?

III. Application

Be aware of how your emotions affect your giving. Take a moment right now, before we give our offering, and see where your heart is. Make sure that as you give today, you choose the Lord over your money. The way to quash greed is to give, and trust in God to provide.

We often encourage people new to our church to give to another charity if you don't yet trust us to handle your gifts properly. The point is to learn to give with a cheerful heart. When you realize this church wants you to be blessed and learn the joy of giving, you'll understand why we encourage you to give.

Week 39: Five Love Languages

I. Attention Getter

There are five major ways that we give and show love. Raise your hand if you have heard of the book "The Five Love Languages" by Gary Chapman. This book talks about those five different ways that everyone gives and receives love. I am going to read them off and I want you to raise your hand when I get to the one that sounds like you.

1. Gift Giving: You give and receive love by sharing gifts with people.
2. Words of Affirmation: You give and receive love by kind words of encouragement.
3. Physical Touch: You give and receive love by hugs and physical touch.
4. Acts of Service: You give and receive love by doing things for other people.
5. Quality Time: You give and receive love by spending time with those you love.

It's great to be self-aware and know the language of love you speak, and especially beneficial to be able to recognize the way others express love toward you. Often we fail to recognize when others are indeed showing us love, because they show it in their own love language and we only want to receive love in ours.

II. Scripture

I Corinthians 13:1-3 says, "If I could speak all the languages of earth and of angels, but didn't love others, I would only be a noisy gong or a clanging cymbal. If I had the gift of prophecy, and if I understood all of God's secret plans and possessed all knowledge, and if I had such faith that I could move mountains, but didn't love others, I would be nothing. If I gave everything I have to the poor and even sacrificed my body, I could boast about it; but if I didn't love others, I would have gained nothing."

We show love to people who are important to us. We give gifts, do acts of service, spend quality time, express affirming words, or give physical touch to people like our kids, our family, our spouse, our friends, and most importantly, to God. Giving is one way that we show God that we love Him, and trust Him to lead our lives.

III. Application

Today as we give, we are touching on all five of our love languages.

1. We are here spending quality time with the Lord.
2. We give our money and our heart.
3. We get out of our seats and give as an act of service.
4. The physical touch we can do is by holding our giving in our hand as a point of contact.
5. Our prayer and worship to Him are words of affirmation. Let's give in love today.

Week 40: Levels of Giving

I. Attention Getter

(I do current research on who the current top three richest people in America. I will name them starting at the third richest, and working my way up to the richest. I ask the congregation to call out how much they think they are worth. Then, I tell the reported net worth of each individual.)

Imagine what it would be like to be that wealthy. Most of us fantasize about how we would spend that kind of money. If you're not rich, it sounds great to be rich. You'd be surprised how much rich people actually give to charitable purposes. In fact, many wealthy people believe that they do better financially because of their charity, not despite it. We say things like, "Well, if I had that much money it would be easy to give big to charity."

II. Scripture

Mark 10:17-22 says, "As Jesus was starting out on His way to Jerusalem, a man came running up to Him, knelt down, and asked, 'Good Teacher, what must I do to inherit eternal life?' 'Why do you call me good?' Jesus asked. 'Only God is truly good. But to answer your question, you know the commandments: "You must not murder. You must not commit adultery. You must not steal. You must not testify falsely. You must not cheat anyone. Honor your father and mother." 'Teacher,' the man replied, 'I've obeyed all these commandments since I was young.' Looking at the man, Jesus felt genuine love for him. 'There is still one thing you haven't done,' He told him. 'Go and sell all your possessions and give the money to the poor, and you will have treasure in Heaven. Then come, follow me.' At this, the man's face fell, and he went away sad, for he had many possessions."

You may think that if you had a lot of money, it would easy to give. The truth is, no matter how much money we have, it is always challenging to give.

There are three different levels of giving the Bible talks about: A *Tithe*, which is 10% that goes to the place that is feeding your spiritually, like your local church. *Offerings*, which is to give a little of what you have to help someone out. And E*xtravagant Giving,* which is giving above what makes sense. This will test our hearts the most.

Our tithes and offerings demonstrate sowing and reaping in this life, an extravagant gift lays up treasure in eternal life. All of these levels of giving are a blessing to the recipient and return to be a blessing to you, the giver. But our hearts are so often more attached to what we have than what we may receive by giving.

III. Application

Jesus may not ask you to give all you have away to follow Him, but will you obey if He asked you to give a little? Is your heart more attached to what you have than what He can bring you? We aren't giving everything that we have today. But we can challenge ourselves to consider what you are giving and if we're interested in greater blessing through faithfulness to Jesus. All of us can give an offering or a tithe, and we can all go to the next level in our giving.

Week 41: The Special Guest Offering

I. Attention Getter

(This lesson is for a day when you want to bring in a special guest, missionary, or project, and give them a special offering. I like to interview them in front of the congregation. I will bring them up and ask them three questions.)

1. Can you tell us a little bit about what you are doing.?
2. What is a specific financial need that we can help you with? Or how much do you still need to raise?
3. What is one practical thing you need that we can pray for?

II. Scripture

Romans 15:25-29 reminds us: "But before I come, I must go to Jerusalem to take a gift to the believers there. For you see, the believers in Macedonia and Achaia have eagerly taken up an offering for the poor among the believers in Jerusalem. They were glad to do this because they feel they owe a real debt to them. Since the Gentiles received the spiritual blessings of the Good News from the believers in Jerusalem, they feel the least they can do in return is to help them financially. As soon as I have delivered this money and completed this good deed of theirs, I will come to see you on my way to Spain. And I am sure that when I come, Christ will richly bless our time together."

As I read this scripture I am reminded that we are still the New Testament church. We are still sharing our resources with faithful partners somewhere else around the world who will do a work that we can't do ourselves.

This is completely biblical, and the way God will multiply our efforts to advance His Kingdom. Thank God for calling individuals to go to the world, and thank God for giving us the opportunity to support these brave people with our prayers and our finances.

We will not only be blessed for sharing this mission, but we all get to partake of the Heavenly reward one day. Many of you here, today met Jesus while attending this church. But long before you ever came, someone far away was praying and giving so this church could be planted. You and I get to be a part of our guest's mission so that others will come to know Jesus through your faithfulness and theirs.

III. Application

(I have the congregation stand and repeat three things:

1. The first name of the guest.
2. A financial goal they are looking to meet.
3. One practical thing that we can be in prayer for.

I have them repeat these three things because I want them to remember them when they are in prayer over the next week. Then I pray over the guest and I pray for those specific three things before we pray over the general offering.)

Week 42: Financial Miracles

I. Attention Getter

All of us go through times when we need a financial miracle. A miracle is defined as "a surprising and welcome event that is not explicable by natural or scientific laws and is therefore considered to be the work of a divine agency. I want to encourage you today, and share a few stories of financial miracles from the Bible.

John 21 tells the story of the disciples fishing, and Jesus told them to cast their nets on the other side of the boat, and their nets will be filled with fish.

Here's another:

II. Scripture

II Kings 4:1-6 tells us: "One day the widow of a member of the group of prophets came to Elisha and cried out, 'My husband who served you is dead, and you know how he feared the Lord. But now a creditor has come, threatening to take my two sons as slaves.' 'What can I do to help you?' Elisha asked. 'Tell me, what do you have in the house?' 'Nothing at all, except a flask of olive oil,' she replied. And Elisha said, 'Borrow as many empty jars as you can from your friends and neighbors. Then go into your house with your sons and shut the door behind you. Pour olive oil from your flask into the jars, setting each one aside when it is filled.' So she did as she was told. Her sons kept bringing jars to her, and she filled one after another. Soon every container was full to the brim. 'Bring me another jar,' she said to one of her sons. 'There aren't any more.' he told her. And then the olive oil stopped flowing.When she told the man of God what had happened, he said to her, 'Now sell the olive oil and pay your debts, and you and your sons can live on what is left over.'

I Kings 17:8-16 tells the story of Elijah, the prophet visiting a widow during a famine. She only had enough oil and flour to make one small cake for her and her son before all the food was gone. Elijah told her to feed him first, and when she did, their oil and flour lasted until the end of the famine.

All of these stories are financial miracles.

In Matthew 17:24, Jesus tells Peter to catch a fish and look in its mouth to find the money necessary to pay their taxes. In this story we actually see Jesus multiply money. God will multiply whatever you need.

(I always tell a financial miracle of my own as well.)

There are three things that all these stories, and many more in the Bible have in common.

1. They all started with someone in need.
2. That person in need was asked to do something that might not have made sense and they *obeyed.*
3. What they had multiplied before their eyes.

III. Application

If you need a miracle, you need your finances to multiply or be raised from the dead. First, serve the Lord with what you have. Peter gave up his family business to follow Jesus, and the widow gave her last flour to feed Elijah. Be obedient in your giving, and you will see a miracle happen in your finances.

Week 43: Unity

I. Attention Getter

How many of you have been in an Escape Room? In an Escape Room, it takes all the brains and talents in the room to figure out all of the riddles and puzzles in order to gain the escape codes. No one is unnecessary; everyone has something to contribute.

In a work environment, everyone contributes to the overall success of the organization. If the boss gave a directive, but everyone did their own thing, chaos would ensue. When all the participants know that they are working toward the same goal, success is within reach, because there is unity. Unity is blessing.

II. Scripture

Acts 2:42-47 says, "All the believers devoted themselves to the Apostles' teaching, and to fellowship, and to sharing in meals (including the Lord's Supper), and to prayer. A deep sense of awe came over them all, and the Apostles performed many miraculous signs and wonders. And all the believers met together in one place and shared everything they had. They sold their property and possessions and shared the money with those in need. They worshiped together at the Temple each day, met in homes for the Lord's Supper, and shared their meals with great joy and generosity, all the while praising God, and enjoying the goodwill of all the people. And each day the Lord added to their fellowship those who were being saved."

What an amazing and miraculous thing that happened here. They were all in unity and blessing poured forth. Everyone had what they needed, and there was a spirit of generosity. Did you know that according to the national average only 20% of the members in any given church contribute financially? Even in churches that look like they are well off, nearly 80% of its attendees are content to participate in and enjoy the ministries without any responsibility for support of the church programs. Yet, many churches are still expected to help the needy, support missions, pay the staff, and expand to meet the needs of the community.

III. Application

The Apostles were giving because they were all in unity, one accord. The believers were all committed to following Christ, preparing for His return, and demonstrating the love of God to the world. And the Bible said, "There were no needs among them."

Can you imagine what it would be like to live with other believers in complete unity? That was a miracle because I don't think it has ever happened since then.

When we are in unity with one another and with Christ, we *want* to do His word, meet the felt needs of others, and support the church where we all grow together. Could you imagine what would be possible if everyone gave according to what they had? There would never be a natural disaster, a family in distress, a missions project we couldn't fund.

Giving is not about your money, but it is about your heart. It's about an attitude toward the Lord. Let's give Him our heart, and be in unity with each other.

Week 44: Faith

I. Attention Getter

Today I want to talk about giving in faith. When we exercise faith, it requires that we believe in something we can't see. I want to read to you my Top 10 list of things that exist but you can't see. (I start with number 10 and work my way up to number one.)

1. Atoms
2. Radio Waves
3. Wind
4. Dark Matter
5. Anti-Matter
6. Air
7. Ultraviolet Light
8. Gravity
9. Infrared
10. Quantum Particles

Scientists have no trouble believing in these things, because they have the experience, the proper tools to study them, and they make it their life's work to know these subjects more. It would be foolish for those who've never studied these elements of our universe to say they don't exist just because we can't see them.

Today we are talking about faith. Some people think that faith is believing in a fairy tale, or pretending something is there that isn't there. The truth is: people of faith have the experience, the proper tools for study, and we make our life's pursuit to know the things of God more thoroughly. It would be foolish for those without sufficient experience to say that God does not exist because we don't see Him.

Faith is believing in something that you can't see, but it is very real, and there is enough evidence to proceed into further study and exploration.

II. Scripture

Hebrews 11:1 says "Faith shows the reality of what we hope for; it is the evidence of things we cannot see."

This scripture says even when I can't see clearly, I can believe God will work it out, and this moment is when I am actually *in* faith, *and* that faith is pleasing to Him. We get no credit for faith when we can see everything in front of us.

We work on our faith daily, right? I have found that for most Christians, we find it easier to believe God for everything in a general sense, but we draw the line when it comes to believing He has a plan for our money.

We ask for healing for a loved one, or we pray for Him to watch over us on the interstate. We ask Him to give us a better job, but we won't start tithing because we think we can't afford it. People ask the pastor for counseling for so many subjects, but if he tries to teach on finances, they think he's trying to take something from them.

It's a matter of faith. To trust that when you give, it will be given back to you as the Bible says. You may not see how it works, but anyone with the right experience and proper tools for research has discovered powerful truths about blessing as real as the atoms that make up your very body.

III. Application

Today I want to challenge you to have faith, based on the evidence in God's Word. Put it into the laboratory of your life, and watch the way God proves Himself to you when you give. Just as you know there is wind, air, gravity, and atoms, know that

God will take care of you when you give to Him. Have faith.

Week 45: Financial Upkeep

I. Attention Getter

(I ask the congregation to call out to me things around the house that need upkeep. They will call out things like: plumbing, drains, cleaning, electrical, air conditioner.)

Wouldn't life be easier if we didn't have to do upkeep on anything? Even a car needs upkeep. Brakes, tires, oil change, the list goes on and on. In fact the value of a house or car determines the cost of the upkeep. The more we have, the more upkeep it requires.

II. Scripture

Proverbs 14:4 says that "Without oxen a stable stays clean, but you need a strong ox for a large harvest."

I love this verse. It's very funny to me. Most of us don't have oxen for our work, but we have cars now. The point is that in order to do some things that are necessary, you're going to have extra work, and quite often some messes to clean. It would be nice to have a clean barn with no animal smell or manure to shovel, but a big, smelly ox makes the harvest possible and more efficient.

We all want to drive a nice car, but if you want it to stay nice, you better plan on oil changes, new tires, regular upkeep. And you should start saving for when that nice car needs to be replaced.

III. Application

Your valuable assets in life don't take care of themselves. They require care. You have to take care of your finances. You have upkeep to do in your finances, just like you have to do for your house, your car, and your job.

Take a look at your finances this week. Sit down, and take inventory of what you have. Clean out what you don't need. Get out that box of receipts you've been stashing for later, reconcile your accounts, clear the mess, and maybe even shovel the manure.

Be faithful to keep up with what God has given you, and you will be trusted with more.

Week 46: Thanksgiving

I. Attention Getter

(I either tell a firsthand account of a rescue story or show a dramatic short one minute video of someone being rescued.)

After watching this video, or hearing this story, do you think the person being rescued was grateful? Do you think there is enough money in the world to repay the hero for what they did? No. The person that was rescued has a choice to make. They could only focus on how close to death they came, and choose to never leave the house again. But instead of thinking about what could have happened, they can be grateful that was not the end of the story. Gratitude is a powerful force in our lives. When you recognize that someone had a positive impact on who you are, and where you are, you'll be grateful for what they've done.

II. Scripture

Luke tells a moving story about a notorious woman who had been forgiven of her sins by Jesus. She came into the house where Jesus sat as the guest of a religious leader. She anointed Jesus with expensive perfume, crying tears on his feet, and drying them with her hair.

Luke 7:44-48 says, "Then He turned to the woman and said to Simon, 'Look at this woman kneeling here. When I entered your home, you didn't offer me water to wash the dust from my feet, but she has washed them with her tears and wiped them with her hair. You didn't greet me with a kiss, but from the time I first came in, she has not stopped kissing my feet. You neglected the courtesy of olive oil to anoint my head, but she has anointed my feet with rare perfume. I tell you, her sins—and they are many—have been forgiven, so she has shown me much love. But a person who is forgiven little shows only little love.' Then Jesus said to the woman, 'Your sins are forgiven.'"

We have all been forgiven *much*. Take a moment as you prepare your offering today. You might have a check, or it might be some cash, or if you give online, grab an offering envelope as a point of contact. Today, we can't come to Jesus and wash His feet. What we can do is be obedient, we can give as an act of gratitude. I want you to write down something that you are grateful to the Lord for in your finances. It might simply be that you have a job, or that you have a comma in your bank balance. Write down something He's done to provide for you, and then put it with your gift.

III. Application

A hero is always deserving of a reward. There is never a reward big enough for what heroes do, but they always deserve gratitude from those they have rescued. We can never repay God for what He has done for us, but we can show Him our love and appreciation. This week is Thanksgiving, so practice thankfulness as you gather with loved ones.

Week 47: Heavenly Riches

I. Attention Getter

I want to share a joke with you. There once was a rich man who was near death. He began to pray that he might be able to take some of his wealth with him. An angel appeared and informed the man that God had decided to allow him to take one suitcase with him. This made the rich man happy, and he filled a large suitcase with gold bars. Soon afterward, he died and showed up at the gates of Heaven. St. Peter, seeing the suitcase, said, "Hold on, you can't bring that in here." The man explained to St. Peter that he had permission, and asked him to verify his story with the Lord. Sure enough, St. Peter checked it out, came back and said, "You're right. You are allowed one carry-on bag, but I'm supposed to check its contents before letting it through." St. Peter opened the suitcase to inspect the worldly items that the man found too precious to leave behind and exclaimed, "You brought pavement?"

I love this joke, it sums up the old saying, "You can't take it with you." Of course, we don't believe that St. Peter will meet you at the gate, We don't believe God will change His rules for entry, and the Bible says there is a "street" of pure gold in the New Jerusalem. The point is, you can't take worldly valuables with you. However, there is something we can do to store up Heavenly riches. Let's look at the following scripture.

II. Scripture

I Timothy 6:17-19 tells us, "Teach those who are rich in this world not to be proud and not to trust in their money, which is so unreliable. Their trust should be in God, who richly gives us all we need for our enjoyment. Tell them to use their money to do good. They should be rich in good works and generous to those in need, always being ready to share with others. By doing this they will be storing up their treasure as a good foundation for the future so that they may experience true life."

There are things that we value highly on Earth that would be virtually worthless in Heaven. Power, wealth, worldly success, prestige. These are things that humans strive to achieve, yet God is looking for humility, generosity, compassion, caring for those in need, obedience, and faith. Let me state this clearly: you cannot earn salvation or Heaven by being a good person. We believe that we are saved by faith in Christ alone. *And* the person who is saved by Christ will demonstrate these acts of goodwill toward others. Collecting power, prestige, success, wealth will be like carrying gold to a place that treats it like pavement. The good works you do here are like a savings account in Heaven.

III. Application

I would like to challenge you this week. Look around for ways to do good works. Who can you be generous to, and is there someone that you can share with? This is what is truly important. Let's give to the Lord, and know our reward will be in Heaven.

Week 48: Faking It

I. Attention Getter

(I bring up a volunteer from the congregation. I have a real dollar bill and I have a color copy of a dollar bill. I ask them to close their eyes. I tell them that I am going to hold them up one at a time for them to smell. Then I ask them which one was the real dollar bill, and which one was the fake.)

Most people can tell just by the smell of a monetary bill which is real, and which is fake.

When you really think about it, there's not much intrinsic value in this small piece of paper called a dollar. What makes it truly valuable is that it's backed up by the U.S. Department of Treasury. When stores, shops, banks, or individuals see the government stamp, the specific designation, and the signature of the proper authority, the bill is recognized as an item of value and backed up by the government.

II. Scripture

I John 5:1-3 says, "Everyone who believes that Jesus is the Christ has become a child of God. And everyone who loves the Father loves His children, too. We know we love God's children if we love God and obey His commandments. Loving God means keeping His commandments, and His commandments are not burdensome."

How do you know a true follower of Christ from a fake one? It's usually found in the fruit of their life. You can fake your love for God. Anyone can claim they follow Jesus, but a true follower is one to practices what they preach. If you love Him you want to keep His commandments, if you don't love Him, you don't care about what He said.

We may not always be experts on telling the genuine from the counterfeit. And it's not really our job to judge. God is the one who knows the genuine article. The Bible says "He knows every thought and intent of our heart." But you can be sure that the genuine follower of Christ is backed up by the very authority of Heaven.

In Matthew 7:21, Jesus said "Not everyone who calls me Lord will enter the Kingdom of Heaven. It will be the one who does the Will of My Father."

III. Application

We are gathered here today to worship Jesus with our lives. We value His Word, and we love His instruction. We give because we love Him, and want to obey His commandments. It is often quoted, "You can give without loving, but you can't love without giving." Today, we give as an act of love for God, for His command, and to honor one another as we share in fellowship.

Week 49: Ask

I. Attention Getter

(Find a happy husband in the congregation, and ask these questions the following questions.)

"What is the single most important question you have ever asked your wife?" (They will usually say when they proposed marriage.

"What was her answer? (Obviously, she said yes.)

"Did you have some level of confidence that she would say yes?"

Why?"

The reason the husband knew that the wife would say yes is because they had spent time together in a relationship. He knew her, and she knew him. They trusted each other and had a confidence in each other.

II. Scripture

I John 5:14-15 reminds us, "And we are confident that He hears us whenever we ask for anything that pleases Him. And since we know He hears us when we make our requests, we also know that He will give us what we ask for."

This verse isn't a carte blanche promise of a blank check from God. It is an assurance that we are in a meaningful, loving, caring relationship with the King of the Universe. The more you know Him, the more He is able to reveal His heart with you, the greater your confidence in His ability to care for you.

We can have confidence and faith that we can ask God for what we need. We all have something that we need. Jesus instructed His disciples to pray "Give us this day our daily bread." You're not being presumptuous to ask your Heavenly Father to provide.

A husband and wife who spend significant time together know each other so well, they can know what is ok to ask, and what would be inappropriate. As you grow in faith, you'll know God always hears you pray. You'll know what pleases Him, and you'll know what requests to make. He loves you. Ask Him.

III. Application

Today let's ask Him for what we need. We know that He is going to hear us, and we can be confident that He will give us what we need.

Week 50: Christmas Spending

I. Attention Getter

(I hold up a wrapped present and then I have the congregation finish this sentence:)

"Jesus is the reason for the ________. " (Season.)

What a great season for sharing with those that we love. Families gather together, decorations give notice of the celebration. Feasts are prepared, gifts are exchanged, and all is right with the world.

Gifts are often the central focus of the holiday. We give presents to each other to show love, as Jesus Christ was God's present to the world that He loved. Giving gifts at Christmas should not be about how much money we spend, but about showing genuine love to each other. Too many people overspend at Christmas, and put themselves in a bad financial situation for the rest of the year.

I want to show you where the tradition of giving gifts at Christmas began.

II. Scripture

Matthew 2:11-12 tells us, "They entered the house and saw the child with his mother, Mary, and they bowed down and worshiped Him. Then they opened their treasure chests and gave Him gifts of gold, frankincense, and myrrh. When it was time to leave, they returned to their own country by another route, for God had warned them in a dream not to return to Herod."\

In this part of the Christmas story we see the Magi, or "wise men" who were led by a star to the newborn King, giving gifts to honor Him. Here is what I want you to see, they gave expensive gifts to baby Jesus. To a poor carpenter's family it must have been an enormous treasure.

However, they did not expend all of their resources. They had enough for their journey, plus enough to take a detour home. They had something left to get themselves back home. They would need food for the journey, places to stay, water and food for their camels, and plenty for any surprises they might meet along the way. They were wise.

It's wonderful to share gifts with our loved ones, but we cannot justify going into debt for a holiday celebration, and jeopardizing our resources for the rest of the year.

III. Application

This season, be wise with your spending. Set limits on your spending. Yes, give gifts, but make sure you have something left over. Don't give everything away or put yourself in a financial bind. Give with the heart of the season and follow the wisdom of the wise men. Jesus was born to be the sacrifice for our sins. He paid the ultimate debt for us so we don't have to live in debt.

Week 51: No Strings Attached-Christmas

I. Attention Getter

(I like to take a small gift card, and wrap it up in a box. Then I tie a really long ribbon or string around it. I will ask the congregation this question: "Who would like a present? Then I throw the gift out with the string still attached. I keep ahold of the string, even after someone catches the gift.)

Okay if you want to keep the present then I need you to wash my car every week for the next two years. Would you do that?"

(When they say no, take the gift back, pick out someone else and do it again. The third person I pick out I don't give them a condition to keeping the gift. I simply cut the string and let them have the gift.)

Most people at some time in their life have received a gift that came with strings attached. You knew there was a condition or an expectation behind the gift. Ask yourself, "Have I ever given a gift to someone with a string attached, even if I thought I didn't I realized later I had an expectation of that person?"

A gift with a condition is not a true gift. A true gift is something of value shared with someone you value, with no expectation of thanks or reciprocation.

II. Scripture

Matthew 2:11-12 says, "The wise men gave gifts to baby Jesus without any strings attached. They gave gold, frankincense, and myrrh and never asked for political favor, future advantage, or anything in return. They didn't even ask for a blessing. They gave without expecting anything in return, recognizing the value of the young child as significant to the world."

John 3:16 says "For God so loved the world, that He gave His only begotten Son, that whosoever believes in Him would not perish, but have everlasting life."

God gave us all a gift we could never deserve or earn.

III. Application

As you go through this Christmas season and you are giving to charities and to loved ones, check your heart and your motive. Make sure that you don't have a hidden expectation. Even if it is the expectation of a great reaction to a gift. Give something of value to someone you value, and you'll be showing the love of Christ.

Week 52: End of Year Giving New Years

I. Attention Getter

(I put up a photo of a storage unit or a storage pod in a driveway. Then, I ask the congregation to call out things that might be stored in a storage unit or pod. Answers may be antiques, extra furniture, old car, old clothes, keepsakes, etc.)

Today's storage units are usually filled with items that no longer fit in our houses. Most storage units are a waste of money, but we keep things because we can't stand to part with things, even though we don't use them anymore. In ancient times, storehouses were kept for sustaining the future. That's right. They were like massive savings accounts. Crops were kept after the harvest and stored into barns to last the rest of the year or longer.

II. Scripture

Malachi 3:10-12 says, "'Bring all the tithes into the storehouse so there will be enough food in my Temple. If you do,' says the Lord of Heaven's Armies, 'I will open the windows of Heaven for you. I will pour out a blessing so great you won't have enough room to take it in. Try it. Put me to the test. Your crops will be abundant, for I will guard them from insects and disease. Your grapes will not fall from the vine before they are ripe,' says the Lord of Heaven's Armies. 'Then all nations will call you blessed, for your land will be such a delight,' says the Lord of Heaven's Armies."

This verse is talking about bringing tithes into the storehouse. What is the storehouse God is referring to? He is referring to the temple where they worshipped Him. Here is where sacrifices were made for sin, here is where the people communed with God, and here is where blessing was pronounced for their lives when they demonstrated obedience to God.

It is completely biblical for you to bring your tithe here to this storehouse, your local church. This is meant to be *your* local storehouse for the Lord. It is where you hear God's Word, where you make your commitments to serve the Lord, and where God chooses to bless you at this season in your life.

The greatest part of God's promise in Malachi is that when you take God's dare to bring your tithes into the storehouse, you are pouring into Heaven's savings account. It's not the pastor's idea, or the church's plan to get your money. It is God's idea to provide for the needs of His people. That provision includes enough to live, enough to give, and enough for your future.

III. Application

Today is your last chance to give to the storehouse for your charitable giving for the year. We give to be obedient, *and* the U.S. government allows you to receive a write-off for giving to charity. That's a double blessing. You are giving to God's storehouse, and as the scripture pointed out you will be blessed.

Shannon Pawlak is an author, wife, mom to two grown daughters, Hannah & Selah, non-profit executive, corporate consultant, professional musician, worship pastor, and certified life coach. She earned her B.A. in Music from the University of Illinois, married her husband Sammy in 1994, and together they planted God's House Orlando Church in 2003.

Made in the USA
Monee, IL
04 November 2026

67382839R10079